A REMNANT IN CRISIS

A REMNANT
IN
CRISIS

JACK W. PROVONSHA

REVIEW AND HERALD® PUBLISHING ASSOCIATION
HAGERSTOWN, MD 21740

The author assumes full responsibility for the accuracy of all facts and quotations as cited in this book.

Unless otherwise indicated, all Scripture texts are from the *Holy Bible, New International Version.* Copyright © 1973, 1978, 1984, International Bible Society. Used by permission of Zondervan Bible Publishers.
Bible texts credited to Anchor are from *Genesis (Anchor Bible)*, translated and edited by E. A. Speiser. Copyright © 1964 by Doubleday & Company, Inc.
Bible texts credited to Phillips are from J. B. Phillips: *The New Testament in Modern English*, Revised Edition. © J. B. Phillips 1958, 1960, 1972. Used by permission of Macmillan Publishing Co., Inc.

This book was
Edited by Richard W. Coffen
Designed by Bill Kirstein
Cover design by Helcio Deslandes
Cover photo by Richard Kaylin/Allstock
Typeset: 11.7/13.7 Clearface

PRINTED IN U.S.A.

98 97 96 95 94 93   10 9 8 7 6 5 4 3 2 1

Library of Congress Cataloging in Publication Data
Provonsha, Jack W.

  A remnant in crisis / Jack W. Provonsha.
    p.   cm.
  1. Seventh-day Adventists—United States. 2. Adventists—United States.
3. Church renewal—Seventh-day Adventists. I. Title.
BX6154.P76 1993   92-41459
286.7'32'09045—dc20   CIP

ISBN 0-8280-0698-9

Contents

Introduction

Some years ago I had the privilege of transporting H.M.S. Richards, Sr., to his home in Glendale, California. The Seventh-day Adventist Church was then at the height of what some called its "FDR Crisis" (not Franklin Delano Roosevelt, but Ford, Davenport, Rea). It was a fairly stormy period in our history, with three major issues confronting us at about the same time. I turned to Elder Richards (he has always been Mr. Adventist to me) and asked, "Elder Richards, what is all this doing to you?" I assumed that it would be fairly traumatic for him to come to the end of a long, fruitful career only to find the church he served and dearly loved in turmoil.

He paused for a long moment and then responded, "Nothing."

How can this be? I thought. *Surely he doesn't understand or is avoiding the question.*

Then he gave his reason. "I've seen it all before."

He was right regarding the FDR issues. None of them was truly novel—different times, different places, different faces, but the same issues. (It is said that if one lives long enough one will get to see everything twice.) However, one thing *was* different—terribly different. Perhaps Elder Richards' work or his age insulated him. What is profoundly different is the crisis of identity that the First World Seventh-day Adventist Church currently faces.

Because of my concern for this crisis I have written this book. Of course, I have no idea whether this book will make a difference. (Who reads books in these days of audio and video cassettes?) Helpful or not, I have felt compelled to write.

Please accept it for what it is—a book written primarily for Seventh-day Adventists by a loyal, fourth-generation Adventist who is deeply sensitive to the changes that have taken place in his church during the past half century. Individuals not of our fellowship are, of course, welcome to read what I have written here. It may provide them with a measure of understanding of the roots, development, struggles, and present complex character of the Seventh-day Adventist Church.

To understand Adventism is not nearly as easy as it was even 50 years ago when other—mainly long-established—churches could, with a cavalier wave of the hand, dismiss the Adventist Church as an insignificant, heretical sect or a cult. During the 1950s Walter Martin, a recognized authority on religious cults, put out the Evangelical welcome mat for Adventists based on theological changes that he came to believe the church had made at its highest leadership levels. As he listened later to other voices, however, including the voices of furor that greeted *Seventh-day Adventists Answer Questions on Doctrine* (1957), the book that grew out of his conversation with Adventist leaders, he began to have second thoughts. These continued until his untimely death in 1989.

What Dr. Martin apparently failed to discern clearly was that by the 1980s a number of voices purported to speak for Adventism. The church was developing the signs of pluriformity that other American churches were also displaying: traditionalists on the one hand, liberals on the other, and a host of poorly defined centrists in the middle. Currently another wave, with charismatic enthusiasm, is lapping on Adventist shores—the so-called celebration movement. This wave may not yet truly be called "charismatic," because those involved do not exhibit classic glossolalia. Nevertheless, they do possess many of the other accoutrements of Pentecostalism, including its worship forms and mind-set.

The tensions that have developed in Adventism because of this pluriformity are not unique to the Adventist Church. They are, however, heightened in Adventism compared with other analogous movements by the exclusive intensity with which Adventists, at least in the past, have stressed their "peculiarity" as a "called" people.

More than most other denominations, from the very beginning Seventh-day Adventists have perceived themselves as "special." In retrospect some of this seems a little paranoid, but the facts remain that because of this perception most Adventists at one time felt that they knew exactly who they were: the "remnant," "the people of God," "the true church," with a special message for a special time. They had "the truth." (Understandably, such claims did not always endear them to their Christian neighbors.)

To a great extent the sense of vocation expressed in these words was underscored by the presence of the prophetic figure of Ellen G. White. Not only had God called Adventists into being, but He had also provided inspired guidance as they set about to finish the work to which they had been called, namely to evangelize the world with "the three angels' messages" of Revelation 14.

For insiders this was all fairly heady stuff. They were "God's people" (literally the 144,000 at first), entrusted with God's final message to the world—the whole world—single-handedly. As preposterous as this idea may seem to some of us today, it was a pivotal factor in the truly enormous explosion of energy that sent Adventists all around the world during the past century and a half, actually changing the world in many ways, but in turn being changed by it.

It would be a gross oversimplification to imply that the Adventist sense of specialness was the sole—or even the major—source of that energy. Being an Adventist is not a simple matter, nor is Adventism unique in its being driven by feelings of divine call and mission. Joseph Smith, prophet of the Church of Jesus Christ of Latter-day Saints, claimed to have been informed by his angel Moroni that he should not join any of the religious sects. They were all false. He was to be given "the real thing" with his famous golden plates. Mormons, retaining the sense of corporate vitality such feelings engender, remain today one of the fastest-growing missionary movements in many parts of the world.

Probably all vigorous movements, religious or otherwise, manifest this quality in one way or another. The aegis of such feelings has partly to do with what motivates "true believers" to commit themselves to causes. Eric Hoffer in his book *The True Believer* describes such persons as "craving for a new life—a rebirth—or, failing this, a chance to acquire new elements of pride, confidence, hope, a sense of purpose and worth by an identification with a holy cause. An active mass movement offers them opportunities for both" (p. 12).

Such reasons suggest an element of self-interest, of course. And I would be the last to claim that the founders and preservers of the Adventist movement were always entirely free of self-interest. They may have been candidates for heaven, but they were also citizens of this world—and it sometimes showed. They also lived at a time prone to novelty. Theirs was a world of change and uncertainty, which culminated in a series of events and processes that had disturbed those continuities of history that customarily nourish social stability and order.

Powerfully selective factors were at work in bringing together those particular young people in that special place and time: the Protestant Reformation; the Enlightenment; the discovery of the New World; the colonization of its Eastern seaboard; the weakening of political, economic, and even ecclesiastical ties with the Old World, this latter yielding a babel of new denominational voices largely unknown in Europe; the taming of a wilderness; the birth travail of a new nation; and finally the separatism and the disappointment of the Millerite anticipation of the return of our Lord. All these together finally distilled out a committed few who, while momentarily confused and profoundly depressed, could not shake the conviction that God had been with them in their expectations.

This last straw, the failure of Millerism, put them back, as they say, to square one (which isn't too bad a place to start when you don't know where you are, where you are going, and how to get there from here). Certainly, this was true theologically. They were young and thus possessed the resilience, energy, and adaptability of youth, but there wasn't a professional Bible scholar or theologian among them. About all they had at first were their Bibles, their concordances, their faith, and, as it turned out, Ellen G. White. These sufficed.

In attempting to rebuild with these resources after the Disappointment, it was almost inevitable that they would later be accused by critics of trying to burrow under two millennia and come up in the first century. As indeed they were. That could not really be done, of course, but they were in a position to give it a better try than most. They probably even benefited from their ignorance of the great church councils such as Chalcedon and Nicea and of the conflicts and contributions of theologians like Origen, Augustine, Aquinas, and the others—at least at first. There would be time for refighting those battles later on.

They believed the Bible to be the Word of God, literally. Under the circumstances, perhaps they should not be judged too harshly if sometimes they interpreted the Scriptures with a tinge of the naïveté that is often the hallmark of the self-taught. They had their Bibles. But they had in large measure that other ingredient for a religious movement's vitality—the sense that they had been called by God and that He was in their movement! Had He not vouchsafed His presence with the gift of prophetic guidance? That made all the difference. Without such a sense at the beginning, there would not now even be a Seventh-day Adventist Church, at least one that made a great deal of difference to the world. The obvious corollary to this is that if that sense is ever lost, the church, even if it continues to exist institutionally, may no longer count where and in the way that it is supposed to count. And that's what this book about the Adventist identity crisis is really all about.

As a committed, lifelong Adventist, I find myself concerned and saddened, in a way, by the sentiments expressed in an anonymous article that recently appeared in the in-house publication of the Loma Linda University church. I quote a portion of this article because I am certain that it represents a perspective shared by a significant number of the youth who have grown up through the Adventist educational system and because it makes my main point.

"Why don't you go to church anymore?" That was the question presented to me some time ago by my local church pastor. The candor of the question surprised me, and I was not able to respond intelligently, just a few stumbling "ah, ah, mm's . . ." Today I still do not attend church as often as that pastor would like, but I have had time to reflect upon his question and now have some definite thoughts about it and my Christianity.

To be totally honest, my goal in my spiritual life right now is to be the best Christian I can be. . . . This is quite a shift in my religious goals. I once was on the right track toward becoming a blue-ribbon Seventh-day Adventist. Born into the religion and educated at Adventist schools, I followed all the rules and teachings of the church as well as I could. . . . I worked hard to become the best Adventist I could because I wanted to be saved!

However, as the years passed, wanting to be saved and [being] considered a good Adventist by my family and my peers just did not seem that important to me. . . . It seemed as though one day I woke up and thought *Why am I doing this?*

In particular, I thought about things such as going to church every Sabbath and keeping faithful to the doctrines of the church, and then I asked myself *Why?* Was it because my parents, teachers, and pastors had said it was so for so many years that I just went along because I wanted to be good? Partly. And what was my Adventist education worth? Was I there to become further indoctrinated with Adventist teachings and grow up in a drug-free environment? Partly this, too. But beyond that, I was a Christian and I still want to be one today. I love the Lord and cannot imagine life without Him. And now I begin to refer to my religion as Christianity rather than Adventism, because, after I thought about it for a while, I have come to the realization that having a personal relation with the Lord is uniquely individual and that in my heart I feel more like a Christian than an Adventist (*Dialogue*, October 1991, p. 31).

This brief account clearly captures the essence of the crisis that I believe the Adventist Church now faces. The account is both honest and sensitive and, I suspect, epitomizes how a great many in Adventism (especially the young, well educated, and upwardly mobile) are coming to feel about their church. It is easy to be sympathetic with the sentiments expressed. But the fact remains that it represents a failure on the part of previous generations to pass on the flame to those coming along. The student who wrote these words apparently does not fully understand the "calling" of this people, and we are all in some measure to blame.

Perhaps what the student's comments illustrate best is that faith is not passed on like a well-worn suit of clothes. What was good enough for Father is *not* good enough for me. Each generation stands on the shoulders of its fathers, but each generation must in some ways be a first generation all over again, or it will be denied the greatest inheritance of all—the sense of purpose that is presupposed by the Adventist mission and vocation. If properly oriented and motivated, this sense can be one of the most satisfying expressions of being a Christian. Being an Adventist in spirit and in truth captures the very essence of Christianity. It is not a question of either/or. How did we fail to communicate this to our young author? Let's think about that in the pages that follow.

* * *

A word about credits. I couldn't begin to pay my debts to all the wonderful people inside and outside the Seventh-day Adventist Church who have influenced this book in one way or another. They have touched me at every level of my life: fellow travelers, acquaintances, friends, teachers, colleagues, parishioners, patients, students, Sabbath school class members, even a few worthy critics along the way.

I owe special thanks to my beloved wife, companion, sincere critic, loyal supporter, proofreader, and sounding board—Margaret. She has read every page several times as she looked for split infinitives, scrambled syntax, dangling participles, typos, and misspelled words, all the while enduring without complaining the loneliness of author-widowhood.

I also owe a debt to my two daughters, who have taught me more theology than they will ever know.

As to sources, in almost every case I have used the New International Version when I have quoted from Scripture because I like it, it reads well, and I find it authoritative. I have quoted liberally from Ellen G. White. I make no apology for this. She is my "spiritual mother." She has also been absolutely central to the life and thought of Adventism. This is, after all, a book for Adventists about their church. No one has been more influential in shaping this church than Ellen White. For this reason I have used only her standard works. As interesting as her letters and unpublished materials may be, it is her standard works—*Steps to Christ*, the Conflict of the Ages Series, *Christ's Object Lessons*, the *Testimonies*, and the like—that, being most accessible to ordinary church members, have influenced them most.

I believe in this church, and I want very much to see it succeed in its mission.

I am also worried about it.

So let's get on with it.

CHAPTER ONE

The Times
They Are a-Changin'

I T IS reported that the Greek sage Heraclitus long ago stated, "We step and do not step into the same river twice." Later Cratylus, who is reported to have communicated by crooking his fifth finger, said when he heard Heraclitus' aphorism, "Ha, you can't even step into the same river once." An American author, Thomas Wolfe, expressed the same notion in the title of his novel *You Can't Go Home Again*. Everything changes. Nothing stays the same. From the minutest atomic fragment out to the most distant quasar, all is in motion.

During the Middle Ages this truism was pronounced to be the major argument for the existence of God. Thomas Aquinas in his *Summa Theologica* wrote:

> The existence of God can be proved in five ways. The first and more manifest way is the argument from motion, . . . whatever is moved must be moved by another. If that by which it is moved be itself moved, then this also must needs be moved by another, and that by another again. But this cannot go on to infinity, because then there would be no first mover, ["an infinite regress is repugnant to the human mind"] and, consequently no other mover, seeing that subsequent movers move only inasmuch as they are moved by the first mover; as the staff moves only because it is moved by the hand.

Therefore it is necessary to arrive at a first mover, moved by no other; and this everyone understands to be God (Anton C. Pegis, ed., *The Basic Writings of Saint Thomas Aquinas*, vol. 1, p. 22).

The paradigm within which Aquinas made this statement is, of course, the now long-outmoded view that the basic, or "natural," state of things is "at rest." Since, according to the logical principle of causality, every effect must have a cause that is at least as great or greater than the effect, the effect—in this case, motion—requires a causal mover who is Himself unmoved, God.

Interestingly, exactly the opposite state of things is postulated today. According to modern understanding, if one were to find something at rest, one would have to explain why it was *not* in motion. "In motion" is regarded as the basic, fundamental state.

We have long since come to recognize that it is not possible to prove (or disprove, for that matter) the existence of God. Belief in His existence is a matter of faith—based on evidence to be sure—but falling short of logical "proof." Later we shall explore some of the reasons that this is so. But the fact of universal motion—change—is a matter of commonsense experience for which logical proof is superfluous. To deny it is to play philosophical games. It is as much a fact of human experience as is consciousness itself. It is self-evident.

But if we believe that God is the Creator of everything that is, we shall also have to say that change is not only self-evident but also that it is good because that's the way God made things. God is the author of change. He is a dynamic God. This is the picture of God portrayed by the Holy Scriptures in contrast with Aristotle's Unmoved Mover, the impassible God, who cannot experience emotions, learn anything, or go anywhere.

Many early Christian philosophers believed that if God experienced any of these things, He would be less than perfect. But in the Bible He is the God who creates, comes to visit human beings, repents (whatever that means in reference to God), delays the destruction of Nineveh, changes His mind in response to a human's changed behavior.

Hear Him.

"[O house of Israel] if at any time I announce that a nation or kingdom is to be uprooted, torn down and destroyed, and if that nation I warned repents of its evil, then I will relent and not inflict on it the disaster I had planned. And if at another time I announce that a nation or kingdom is to be built up and planted, and if it does evil in my sight and does not obey me, then I will reconsider the good I had intended to do for it" (Jer. 18:6-10).

As for God's never learning anything new, how shall we understand the following?

Multitudes in the world are witnessing this game of life, the Christian warfare. And this is not all. *The Monarch of the universe* and the myriads of heavenly angels are spectators of this race; they are *anxiously watching to see who will be successful overcomers* and win the crown of glory that fadeth not away. *With intense interest* God and heavenly angels mark the self-denial, the self-sacrifice, and the agonizing efforts of those who engage to run the Christian race (Ellen G. White, *Testimonies for the Church*, vol. 4, pp. 34, 35; italics supplied).

In addition, the writings of Ellen White contain many statements that suggest that the Christian journey is a march rather than an encampment. Note the implications for change in the following.

Whenever the people of God are growing in grace, they will be *constantly obtaining a clearer understanding* of His Word. They will discern new light and beauty in its sacred truths. This has been true in the history of the church in all ages, and thus it will continue to the end. But as real spiritual life declines, it has ever been the tendency to cease to advance in the knowledge of the truth. Men rest satisfied with the light already received from God's Word, and they discourage any further investigation of the Scriptures. They become conservative, and seek to avoid discussion. [See also *Testimonies*, vol. 5, p. 463.]

The fact that there is no controversy or agitation among God's people should not be regarded as conclusive evidence that they are holding fast to sound doctrine. There is reason to fear that they may not be clearly discriminating between truth and error. When no new questions are started by investigation of the Scriptures, when no difference of opinion arises which will set men to searching the Bible for themselves, to make sure that they have the truth, there will be many now, as in ancient times, who will hold to tradition, and worship they know not what (Ellen G. White, *Counsels to Writers and Editors*, pp. 38, 39; italics supplied).

Greater light shines upon us than shone upon our fathers. We cannot be accepted or honored of God in rendering the same service, or doing the same works, that our fathers did. In order to be accepted and blessed of God as they were, we must imitate their faithfulness and zeal—*improve our light as they improved theirs*—and do as they would have done had they lived in our day (*Testimonies*, vol. 1, p. 262; italics supplied).

The Lord has been revealed to us *in ever-increasing light*. Our privileges are far greater than were the privileges of God's ancient people. We have not only the great light committed to Israel, but we have the increased evidence of the great salvation brought to us through Christ (Ellen G. White, *Christ's Object Lessons*, p. 317; italics supplied).

Our responsibility is greater than was that of our ancestors. We are accountable for the light which they received, and which was handed down as an inheritance for us, and we are accountable also for the additional light which is now shining upon us from the Word of God (Ellen G. White, *The Great Controversy*, p. 164).

And finally this statement.

The Word of God presents special truths for every age. The dealings of God with His people in the past should receive our careful attention. We should learn the lessons which they are designed to teach us. But we are not to rest content with them. God is leading out His people step by step. *Truth is progressive.* [As we shall see later, she undoubtedly meant that our perception of "truth is progressive."] The earnest seeker will be constantly receiving light from heaven. What is truth? should ever be our inquiry (*The SDA Bible Commentary*, Ellen G. White Comments, vol. 2, p. 1000; italics supplied).

According to Mrs. White, this is also the shape of things to come.

There [heaven], immortal minds will contemplate with never-failing delight the wonders of creative power, the mysteries of redeeming love. . . . *Every faculty will be developed, every capacity increased. The acquirement of knowledge* will not weary the mind or exhaust the energies. There the grandest enterprises may be carried forward, the loftiest aspirations reached, the highest ambitions realized; and still *there will arise new heights to surmount, new wonders to admire, new truths to comprehend, fresh objects to call forth the powers of mind and soul and body.* . . . And the years of eternity, as they roll, will bring *richer and still more glorious revelations of God* and of Christ. *As knowledge is progressive, so will love, reverence, and happiness increase.* The more men learn of God, the greater will be their admiration of His character (*The Great Controversy*, pp. 677, 678; italics supplied).

It has been said that hell is the place where one climbs to the top of the mountains by great and arduous effort only to discover that there are no more mountains to climb, or where one finds the answers to all of one's questions and there are no more questions. Heaven involves growth and change—or what is heaven for?

This brings us to a subtle but important distinction that must be made between change in and by itself and change that represents growth and development. Earlier we noted God's dynamic relation to His creation, a creation in which nothing stays the same. Nothing? Not quite. There is one exception to the rule of universal motion, an exception that keeps universal change from being just another name for universal chaos.

Along with references to the dynamism of God, there are other texts of Scripture that testify to God's changelessness. The prophet Malachi records the words of God, "I the Lord do not change" (Mal. 3:6), and the writer of Hebrews says of Jesus the incarnate Lord, He is "the same yesterday and today and forever" (Heb. 13:8).

These texts do not imply, however, that God is totally "outside of," "above," or "beyond" His changing universe. No. What they call attention to is that He can relate harmoniously to change precisely because there is a quality in Him that always remains the same even in the midst of change. That quality is His changeless character. With change occurring all around Him, He remains always loving, always just, and always merciful. The remainder of the statement in Malachi says as much: "I the Lord do not change. So you, O descendants of Jacob, are not destroyed." They had good reason to expect destruction, given their rebellious ways, but the Lord remained always loving, always just, and always merciful. You can always depend upon God to do the loving thing, the right thing, and to extend mercy. That's the way He is—even if His loving, just, and merciful actions seem to us at times to be incomprehensible.

This is a point of great importance. Herein lies the distinction between change that is growth and development and change that is merely chaotic. _Growth and development involve continuity._ The tree is not reducible to just its roots, _but_ it is alive and bears fruit because it maintains contact with those roots. That great man of science and letters Sir Isaac Newton once observed that the reason he could see farther than others was because he stood on the shoulders of giants. But this was made possible because of those particular shoulders. Thank God for the shoulders of our giant fathers and mothers in the Adventist Church, which enable us to see farther than they saw. But the greatest disrespect one can show to them is not to move one inch beyond where they stood.

Change is good, but discontinuous change is . . . nothing. Nothing can exist without continuity of some sort—as even the new physics with its chaos theory seems to be telling us. We can speak of a universe instead of a multiverse (or, worse, nothingness) because of the universal character of its Creator and Sustainer. There can be His unity in our diversity, and that's something that a church facing an identity crisis should think about.

What has changed or is changing that constitutes the basis for our crisis of identity? This can be a trivial question or one asked in all seriousness. Be forewarned that this question is not here being asked merely at the superficial level of customs, lifestyle, or even technological development—as consuming as these matters may sometimes seem. Any significance given to these will be mainly as they are indicators of something more substantial.

Changes at the surface level have been truly enormous during this century. The most spectacular of these have been in the area of the management of information, information gathering, storage, retrieval, and communication. The level of technology even a half century ago seems almost from a dark age by comparison.

These changes have affected Seventh-day Adventists just as they have everyone else. My lifetime has spanned many of them. When I was born, Adventist missionaries—like all missionaries—were still reaching their far-flung mission assignments by automobiles of uncertain vintage and dependability, trains, steamships, and finally by oxcarts, foot trails, and the like.

It literally took months for these dedicated workers to receive letters from home, for there were no jumbo jets, no communications satellites, no fax machines. These missionaries went out with the intention of staying there forever. And it sometimes seemed like forever, too, as they struggled to adjust to impossible climates, snakes, vermin, and incomprehensible customs. They suffered from culture shock (they didn't have a name for it then). They studied hard to learn tongue-twisting languages. They became separated from their children when they became old enough to attend secondary school, literally not seeing them again for years.

Finally, if they didn't succumb to one of those dreadful, untreatable tropical diseases, they came home on permanent return to old age in a world that had largely passed them by—a world of new ideas, new habits, and new fashions, where the home church, many of whose members had been making it pretty well in their absence, now seemed worldly and uncaring about its world mission. Experiencing a second dose of culture shock—the shock of reentry—returnees tended to club together with others who had similarly spent their lives, to ease the great emptiness they felt for the ones left behind forever in the mission field.

There are other changes. For one, that White American bwana of former times, throwing his weight around in the Third World, has increasingly outlived his welcome. Strong feelings of anti-colonialism and nationalism, plus higher levels of education among nationals (often gained overseas), and affluence on the part of the upper classes in some of these countries have diminished the influence of and the need for overseas expatriates. This has reduced the stream of eager young missionaries to a mere trickle compared to former times. Those who do go overseas are often short-term specialists of various kinds. Frequently they are retirees who have special skills or maybe college students who are bent on finding adventure and a feeling of worthwhileness as they play at being missionaries for a brief time in distant lands of which they had dreamed as children.

At administrative levels nationals have taken over the reins. Given the demographics of the situation (only a very small percentage of the church's membership now resides in North America), it is only a question of time before a Third World figure with a non-White face sits behind that desk at 12501 Old Columbia Pike, in Silver Spring, Maryland (although it could be a good deal longer before we shall be able to wish *her* well).

Changes that have taken place in the Adventist Church's overseas medical work are a case in point. Time was when Adventists could take great pride in a string of "jewels" throughout the Orient and elsewhere—our missionary hospitals. We were known for our medical institutions the world around. Indeed, it was almost all we were known for in some circles! American State Department officials and tourist agencies would advise American tourists and others, that if they ever had medical needs in far-off places like Bangkok, Rangoon, or Singapore, the place to head for was the nearest Adventist hospital. The local upper classes also knew us well. In some places the Adventist hospital was about the only representation of Western medicine available.

It makes a thrilling story—as do the lives of those marvelous people who made it all possible! But now the paint is peeling. Oh, some of them are doing very well, thank you—a few of them. But Western medicine has been introduced into many of these countries with a vengeance, with government sponsorship. It is not easy for a small, aging missionary hospital to compete with a brand-new showplace down the street, equipped with all the latest medical gadgetry and staffed by nationals who have been superbly trained in the West, and where supplies, including medicines, are state-of-the-art. In some places about all we have going for us is the tender loving care that is always the hallmark of a Christian hospital (it is still a power to be reckoned with), along with an occasional White face to remind people, at least older people, of former days.

The evangelistic outreach of the church has changed even more here in the homeland. Back in those early days most of the church's growth in North America resulted from public evangelistic meetings. The local pastor or a team involving a conference evangelist would prepare for their campaigns by flooding the community with handbills (often lurid), setting up the conference tent in a vacant lot as near to the center of town as possible, putting up eye-catching billboards, and waiting for the crowds they were virtually assured of drawing since theirs was really the only show in town.

The audience was almost certainly churchgoing and Bible-believing. They may have been largely ignorant of what the Bible actually contained, except for the usual familiar stories, but if the evangelist could prove a point from the Bible, it carried conviction. Local, mainly Protestant, ministers might be more or less successful in warning their flocks on Sunday morning against being taken in by these fly-by-night Adventists, even providing alternative interpretations of troublesome proof texts. Some of them might even be foolish enough to engage the evangelist in debate, a debate they couldn't possibly win if they stuck to the King James Version.

Those were the days! (Miriam Wood's delightful book *Those Happy Golden Years* captures the period beautifully.) They were filled with hardship, sometimes, especially for the ministerial intern and his new bride, who were attached to the seasoned evangelist, but they were also days filled with adventure, excitement, and meaning. They were the people of God, the remnant, the true church, out to finish God's work.

I was a ministerial intern toward the close of that period. As a boy I had helped the evangelist when he came to our town. I was barked at by the neighborhood dogs as I passed out the weekly handbills in the territory assigned to me. I helped spread the sawdust that covered the floor of the evangelistic tent, set up the benches or folding chairs, and operated the slide projector with its lurid beasts of Daniel's prophecies. Later I finished the ministerial course at Pacific Union College (we had no seminary as yet) and was taken on as a ministerial intern in Utah, a singing evangelist, no less. Those were World War II years, and we evangelists made vivid use of war newsreels to underscore Armageddon and all that. The war also provided the theme for an eye-catching display in the front window of the vacant store that we had rented for the occasion. There were other evangelistic campaigns in other places, but none stands out quite so clearly in my memory's eye.

And then came television and televangelism, and the world will never again be the same. How'r ya gonna keep 'em down at the forum after they've seen TV? To survive, evangelists had to bow to Hollywood and Madison Avenue like everybody else.

After that came also the Seminary, and seminaries, divinity schools, graduate schools, scholarship, degrees, and higher learning—and greater accuracy and understanding, truth through scholarship rather than authority. And the church grew up and became dull, at least for some who now prefer to sing and to dance. And is this too surprising? No. But surely it is different.

Some would tell us that the difference is mainly in style rather than in substance. Perhaps so. We will want to be sure about that. But for now it does make the point. The times they are a-changin'.

CHAPTER TWO

The Roots of the Crisis

UNDER the guidance of Ellen White, Seventh-day Adventists have always been committed to quality education. Educating our children in our own schools has also always been seen as a way of protecting them from contact with the world. It used to be said of Pacific Union College, nestling in the woodsy environment of Howell Mountain in northern California, that it was 10 miles from any known sin!

It was said in jest, of course. No one anywhere is geographically safe from sin so long as his or her mind remains active, but the point is well taken if we are thinking in terms of our children retaining a connection with the church. Every survey indicates that children who grow up through the Adventist educational system are far more likely to remain Adventists than are those who attend public schools. That is not too surprising. The same can be said for Catholics, Lutherans, or any other group involved in parochial education.

But this is most likely to be the case if the sponsoring denomination perceives this to be one of its main reasons for being involved. Ineffective church-sponsored education is probably little more a guarantee of loyalty to a church than is education in the public sector.

The quality of Adventist education was virtually assured by the active role that Ellen White played in establishing the system. Her insights, as expressed in such books as *Education* and *Fundamentals of Christian Education*, are classics in the field. These and other of her writings, plus her commitment to the Protestant work ethic, underscored by a large amount of hands-on guidance, were pivotal in shaping an extraordinary educational program. As it turns out, one of the most important occasions of hands-on counsel—given in 1910—set the pattern for the whole system. The church leaders were meeting in Mountain View, California, considering, among other things, the future of the medical school, which was then only in embryo. They wrote to her for advice.

Are we to understand, from what you have written concerning the establishment of a medical school at Loma Linda, that, according to the light you have received from the Lord, we are to establish a thoroughly equipped medical school, the graduates from which will be able to take state board examinations and become registered, qualified physicians?

Ellen White replied:

The medical school at Loma Linda is to be of the highest order, because those who are in that school have the privilege of maintaining a living connection with the wisest of all physicians, from whom there is communicated knowledge of a superior order. And for the special preparation of those of our youth who have clear convictions of their duty to obtain a medical education that will enable them to pass the examinations required by law of all those who practice as regularly qualified physicians, we are to supply whatever may be required, so that these youth need not be compelled to go to medical schools conducted by men not of our faith (D. E. Robinson, *The Story of Our Health Message*, pp. 385, 386).

The consequences of that statement have been momentous. By recommending that the medical school achieve full legal and professional standing, Ellen White had also determined by inference (if not by intention) that the feeder-schools (our undergraduate colleges) must also be so qualified, that is, accredited. And, of course, to accredit the higher feeder-schools required seeking accreditation in turn for their feeder-schools, and so on, ad infinitum. With a stroke of her pen Ellen White virtually assured that the entire Adventist educational system would achieve a status at least on a par legally and professionally with other school systems. This, in turn, included the fostering of higher education for faculty, which accreditation requires. (Whether or not those M.A.s and Ph.D.s were initially intended, they were almost inevitable once the M.D. step was taken.)

It was a fateful recommendation in other ways. At least at first, those higher degrees could be obtained only from non-Adventist institutions. The walls of intellectual separation between "insiders" and "outsiders" were irrevocably breached. (Of course, it was not quite that simple. Those walls were already crumbling for other reasons. Being educated in our school system probably encouraged rather than prevented students from discovering those impressive books, journals, and other materials out there.)

This is important to us here because of the part this has played in our identity crisis. The crisis is associated with the relative increase in the educational level of many church members. This could not help modifying the Adventist paradigm or worldview. Things do not look the same through formally-educated eyes.

The crisis is also related to the fact that the process has been uneven. Not everyone has shared in it. Consequently, we have at one end of a very broad spectrum a far greater number of highly trained professionals and academicians than we have a statistical right to expect given our numbers and socioeconomic antecedents. At the other end lie a significant number of individuals who may be gifted but are, for one reason or another, educationally deprived. The situation is not enhanced by the fact that most new converts are won to Adventism from the lower socioeconomic sector. The broadness of the spectrum, while making things interesting, virtually guarantees that tensions will develop.

The increase in general awareness that education brings has also modified the church's vision of its task. Initially that small company had little comprehension of the enormity of the task facing them in world evangelism. Most expected the Parousia within a single generation, based on Jesus' "this generation shall not pass away till all be fulfilled."

Uriah Smith and others even suggested that the final prophecy of the Lord's return, "This gospel of the kingdom will be preached in the whole world as a testimony to all nations, and then the end will come," had already been largely fulfilled in their time by God's providential planting of the message in America. America had gathered representative peoples from all the world to her melting pot—Swedes to Minnesota, Germans to Wisconsin, Italians and Irish to Boston, Orientals to California, Afro-Americans to the South, etc. The prophecy could be fulfilled without our even leaving American shores! Eventually we did get around to sending out our first foreign missionary—J. N. Andrews—to, of all places, Switzerland, the seat of the Reformation! South America, India, Africa, China, the islands of the sea—these would all have to wait for an Adventist presence.

Gradually it began to sink in that the "whole world" was an awfully big place. But the expectation persisted. Nothing was impossible for God. During my childhood I heard my elders discussing whether it displayed a lack of faith in the imminent return to plant fruit trees that wouldn't bear fruit for three to five years or to build substantial church buildings. Eventually, however, many Adventists would be able to identify with the elderly retired church leader I once knew who, while attending a meeting of conference workers, asked for permission to speak. Out of respect for what this elderly gentleman had meant to the cause, this was granted.

He began, "Brethren, when I was a small child I asked my mother when Jesus was coming. She told me, 'In not more than five years, my child.' When I was 10 years of age—five years later—I asked my mother again, and again she said, 'Surely in not more than five years.' When I was 15, I asked my mother again, and she replied just as she had before. And then I was 20 and 25, and still she said, 'In not more than five years, my son.' " The old man continued, his voice quavering with age and emotion, "Now I am old, and my Jesus has not come." As he sat down, the room was very still.

Maranatha, the Lord is coming, does not come as easily to Adventist lips more than a century and a half later as it did early in October of 1844. This is especially true as believers come to understand how unrealistic was that earlier vision of Adventists "finishing the work" by knocking on every door on earth and proclaiming the 27, or whatever, doctrines of the church.

I was at the General Conference session in New Orleans and was as thrilled as anyone as the figures were totaled at the close of the "1000 Days of Reaping." We had actually added almost 2 million souls to our church's membership during the allotted period! It was, unfortunately, something of a letdown to learn afterward that the world's population had increased by 250 million during that same period, a figure equal to the entire population of the United States!

And to compound things, missiologist Ralph Winter has informed us that even today more than half the world's population is not yet culturally prepared to perceive the witness of the gospel. In America itself nearly 70 percent of people know almost nothing about Seventh-day Adventists, even after all those evangelistic efforts and radio and television programs!

To their credit, Adventist global strategists have begun to think in terms of establishing a presence in the "people groups" of earth. But even on these terms it appears that we still have a way to go. Communications technology should help. It is the one thing that is really different about our time. (I personally find Adventist World

Radio a very exciting development. We will face the question of whether we as a denomination are expected to "finish the work" all by ourselves, including what is meant by the expression "finishing the work," a little later on in the book.)

A dawning awareness of the enormity of the task remaining is a major reason for the present identity crisis. A manufacturing firm was attempting to increase the productivity of its assembly-line workers. Efficiency consultants suggested that they try first a covert, gradual increase in the speed of the assembly line. This took place in such small increments that the workers were unaware of it, and they worked faster—up to a point. Eventually, they were overwhelmed and simply gave up. A task has to be at least perceived to be doable before it can enlist our best efforts.

Given the logistics and demographics involved, is the task to which we believed we were called really doable? The world is full of people and is becoming more crowded all the time. Any Western tourist to southern Asia will understand the sentiments expressed by Paul Ehrlich:

> I came to understand it emotionally one stinking hot night in Delhi a few years ago. My wife and daughter and I were returning to our hotel in an ancient taxi. The seats were hopping with fleas. The only functional gear was third. As we crawled through the city, we entered a crowded slum area. The temperature was well over 100, and the air was a haze of dust and smoke. The streets seemed alive with people. People eating, people washing, people sleeping. People visiting, arguing, and screaming. People thrusting their hands through the taxi windows, begging. People defecating and urinating. People clinging to buses. People herding animals. People, people, people, people (*The Population Bomb*, p. 1).

I once asked an Adventist missionary to southern Asia what the contrast between his small Christian congregation and the huge, human anthill of "unsaved heathen" in which he found himself did to him, especially in reference to a "finished work." He was quiet for a long moment and then replied, "I try not to think about it."

A faith that is based entirely on the future is a vulnerable faith, vulnerable to the future turning out other than was anticipated. (E. Stanley Jones says somewhere that the present guarantees the future—the future does not guarantee the present.) We are Adventists. Our identity, life, and meaning are tied up with the expectation of Jesus' imminent return. From the very beginning we have looked for and continue to look for that glorious event. William Miller stated the case for most of our fathers when, after the Great Disappointment, he said in response to the question When is He coming now? "Today, today, and today—until He comes."

But what if He doesn't come in our day? Can a church built on that expectation survive a prolonged delay without losing its sense of meaning and purpose? What happens to an Adventist movement when maranatha becomes a "far-off divine event toward which all creation moves"? And what happens when "belief" becomes merely "believing in believing"?

One other discovery, in addition to the complexity and vastness of the task and its relative lack of completion, has resulted from increasing contact with the world as we moved out of our earlier denominational ghettos. Many "outsiders" turned out to be a much better lot than we expected them to be. During our days of relative exclusiveness, it was always tempting to distinguish saints and sinners by the baubles they wore, the way they were dressed, to what they ate and drank (or didn't), their lifestyles, how they talked, and/or to what church or club they belonged.

With acquaintance, however, one was often surprised by the depth of compassion, honesty, plain decency, and devotion to God displayed by such persons. And, more unsettling, we discovered that they often believed and were witnessing about many of the same things we were. And sometimes they did it better than we! It's a fact. Most of our doctrines we share with other Christians.

It is hard to feel "special" when one discovers that "unspecial" people are stealing his or her best lines! It is enough to cause one to hesitate over whether Adventism is but "one tribe in Israel," rather than Israel itself. Pearl Buck captures the feeling beautifully in *All Under Heaven*:

> He was confounded by the eternal injustice of life. Saints and sinners! He remembered that when traveling once in the far interior of a northern province in China he had come upon a fiery old missionary striding along a stone-paved street older than the streets of Jerusalem. The two White men, each of whom thought himself solitary, stopped, stared, and then embraced each other.
>
> "Come home with me, brother," the old missionary shouted. "The inns are full of fleas and I am the only human being in town who doesn't eat garlic!"
>
> He had accepted the invitation gladly and spent the night in a vast bare mission house, listening to the overflow of that old saint.
>
> "When I get to heaven," the saint had proclaimed with confidence, "I'm going to ask God a question—just one question, mind you!"
>
> His lean old forefinger had wagged at Malcolm while his blue eyes burned. "I'm going to ask God why He didn't make heathen all bad and Christians all good. It would simplify the whole of human life, mind you! As it is—ha!"
>
> "As it is?" Malcolm suggested.
>
> "As it is," the saint declared, "there's no satisfaction in converting a heathen when you find that he was a good

man anyway—none at all! And it's a humiliating thing, brother, but I'll confess it as a Christian and an honest man, and mind you"—the forefinger wagged at him again—"the two aren't always the same thing. My best Christians were once the best heathens in the town. It's no satisfaction, I tell you" (pp. 67, 68).

And we all know the truth of that picture. None of us has either the right or the wisdom to judge another person's fitness for heaven. God, who reads people's hearts, takes into account that this one was born here or there, and He judges integrity according to the light perceived. This does compound our problem of identity, however. Indeed, on these grounds, the claim to be a special people, the remnant, the people of God, seems almost perverse.

(I was once giving a lecture on the Seventh-day Adventist Church to the students and faculty of a large Methodist seminary when, 10 minutes before the bell, a lady seminarian in the front row interrupted me to ask what Adventists mean when they speak of the "people of God." I noted that she had a copy of *Signs of the Times* on her lap. It was not an easy question to answer under such circumstances. I must confess to having given her what amounted to a nonanswer that served mainly to deflect the question.)

How shall we deal with these two destabilizing questions? 1. How is it, if the Adventist Church is God's special people—His true church—that it makes so minimal an impact on the larger world? That is, How is it that the true church is so small a drop in so big a bucket of humanity? 2. How can the "people of God" be so special when there are so many other "special" people in the world?

The current crisis demands an answer. We must give it a try.

CHAPTER THREE

The True Believers

O NE way to approach to the unsettling questions posed at the end of the previous chapter is from the perspective of Christ's "true church," an expression with a long history in Adventism. Most of us, over the years, have thought of Christ's true church in terms of a succession of entities: Israel of old, the church of the New Testament, the "church in the wilderness" during the apostasy of the Dark Ages (the Waldenses, etc.), then the church of the Protestant Reformation, which was finally succeeded by today's standard-bearer, the true, the Seventh-day Adventist Church.

Traditional Adventist evangelists usually presented a sermon on the true church somewhere near the close of their campaigns. Drawing attention to the confusion of religious bodies, each declaring that it had the truth (and thus implying that all the others were false), the "true church" lecture emphasized the marks by which its voice could be singled out of the general denominational babel. These marks usually included its being small in membership (that is, until there were so many of us), a remnant (as in what is left over at the end of a bolt of cloth), commandment-keeping (the Sabbath had already been convincingly presented), world-evangelizing (faithful to the gospel commission), preaching the three angels' messages, and, finally, having the gift of prophecy.

After surveying the "marks," it was not difficult to identify which was the "true church." The evangelist had seen to that. The only question remaining was Are you going to join it? a different kind of question and one a bit more difficult to answer affirmatively.

A series of statements by Ellen White plus some familiarity with Christian church history render the above sequence difficult to maintain. What institutional church, for example, qualifies for the following?

> During ages of spiritual darkness, the church of God has been a city set on a hill. *From age to age, through successive generations,* the pure doctrines of heaven have been unfolding within its borders. Enfeebled and defective as it may appear, the church is the one object upon which God bestows in a special sense His supreme regard. It is the theater of His grace, in which He delights to reveal His power to transform hearts (Ellen G. White, *The Acts of the Apostles*, p. 12; italics supplied).

> The church is God's fortress, His city of refuge, which He holds in a revolted world. . . . *From the beginning, faithful souls have constituted the church on earth. In every age* the Lord has had His watchmen, who have borne a faithful testimony to the generation in which they lived. These sentinels gave the message of warning; and when they were called to lay off their armor, others took up the work. God brought these witnesses into covenant relation with Himself, *uniting the church on earth with the church in heaven (ibid.,* p. 11; italics supplied).

According to Ellen White, the true church is found in strange settings:

> *Even among the heathen* are those who have cherished the spirit of kindness; before the words of life had fallen upon their ears, they have befriended the missionaries, even ministering to them at the peril of their own

lives. *Among the heathen* are those who worship God ignorantly, those to whom the light is never brought by human instrumentality, yet they will not perish. Though ignorant of the written law of God, they have heard His voice speaking to them in nature, and have done the things that the law required. Their works are evidence that the Holy Spirit has touched their hearts, and they are recognized as the children of God (Ellen G. White, *The Desire of Ages*, p. 638; italics supplied).

Outside of the Jewish nation there were men who foretold the appearance of a divine instructor. These men were seeking for truth, and to them the Spirit of Inspiration was imparted. One after another, like stars in the darkened heavens, such teachers had arisen. Their words of prophecy had kindled hope in the hearts of thousands of the Gentile world. . . . *Among those whom the Jews styled heathen* were men who had a better understanding of the Scripture prophecies concerning the Messiah than had the teachers in Israel. There were some who hoped for His coming as a deliverer from sin (*ibid.*, p. 33; italics supplied).

And more nearly our own time:

Notwithstanding the spiritual darkness and alienation from God that exist in the churches which constitute Babylon, the great body of Christ's true followers are still to be found in their communion. There are many of these who have never seen the special truths for this time. Not a few are dissatisfied with their present condition, and are longing for clearer light (*The Great Controversy*, p. 390).

This harmonizes with John's inspired reference to the Word: "The

true light that gives light to every man was coming into the world"
(John 1:9) and with Paul's:

> The wrath of God is being revealed from heaven
> against all the godlessness and wickedness of men who
> suppress the truth by their wickedness, since what may
> be known about God is plain to them, because God made
> it plain to them. For since the creation of the world God's
> invisible qualities—his eternal power and divine
> nature—have been clearly seen, being understood from
> what has been made, so that men are without excuse. . . .
> For it is not those who hear the law who are righteous in
> God's sight, but it is those who obey the law who will be
> declared righteous. (Indeed, when Gentiles, who do not
> have the law, do by nature things required by the law,
> they are a law for themselves, even though they do not
> have the law, since they show that the requirements of
> the law are written on their hearts, their consciences also
> bearing witness, and their thoughts now accusing, now
> even defending them.) (Rom. 1:18-20; 2:13-15).

How shall we recognize these "faithful souls"? Where are they?
Under what banner, name, or title do they worship? What form does
their worship take and in what shrine, church, cathedral, mosque,
temple, tabernacle, synagogue, sanctuary, or desert quiet place? How
does the sign on the outside of their place of worship read? What
organization ties them together and coordinates their mission? Who
are their leaders and from what scriptures do they teach their
children?

These are difficult questions to answer fully. "Faithful souls" may
wear differing labels and live in widely varied cultures, times, and
places. Only God knows them for sure, since they are not distinguish-
able by the usual institutional marks of identity. They are the sheep of
Christ's "other fold." They are known by the Shepherd, and they know

their Shepherd's voice. They are recognized by God for their integrity as He judges integrity. They are the "honest in heart," those who live up to the light they have. They are the "safe to save," safe because they have demonstrated that they will follow the leading of God in the courts of heaven, just as they have attempted to follow Him here on earth.

Theologians and church historians have sometimes referred to these faithful ones under the rubric the "church invisible"—invisible to humans, that is, not to God. They are invisible in the sense of not necessarily conforming to the usual marks of identity. Presumably some could at times come close to what Voltaire (who was branded an infidel more because he was an anti-cleric than because he was an atheist) expounds as his own personal faith in an article in his *Dictionary* under the heading "Theist."

> The theist is a man firmly persuaded of the existence of a supreme being as good as he is powerful, who has formed all things . . . ; who punishes, without cruelty, all crimes, and recompenses with goodness all virtuous actions. . . . His religion is the most ancient and the most widespread; for the simple worship of a God preceded all the systems of the world. He speaks a language which all peoples understand, while they do not understand one another. He has brothers from Pekin to Cayenne, and he counts all the sages for his fellows. He believes that religion consists neither in the opinions of an unintelligible metaphysic, nor in vain shows, but in worship and in justice. To do good is his worship, to submit to God is his creed. The Mohammedan cries out to him, "Beware if you fail to make the pilgrimage to Mecca!"—the priest says to him, "Curses on you if you do not make a trip to Notre Dame de Lorette!" He laughs at Lorette and at Mecca: but he succors the indigent and defends the

oppressed (quoted in Will Durant, *The Story of Philoso-phy*, p. 184).

It is only the "church invisible" made up of "faithful souls in every age" and united with the church in heaven that warrants the title "the true church." Its "books" or "membership rolls" are kept in heaven. Its kingdom is that which Christ said was "not of this world." Membership is based on integrity and compassion, not on material, institutional, or social structures. When one day the "church invisible" becomes visible, we shall discover that it wore a variety of superficial labels.

Will it not be one of the pleasantries of the hereafter to compare notes regarding the earthly identifying marks we wore when God found us: infidel, heathen, Hindu, Buddhist, Muslim, Samaritan, Jew, Christian?

Can we not even see one in that throng who once considered himself a skeptic, yet who was really worshiping God "ignorantly"? There are some conceptions of God, you know, that a person of integrity ought to reject. According to Francis Bacon, it is better to have no conception of God at all than to have a conception that is unworthy of Him. He quotes Plutarch as saying, "I would much rather that men would say that there is no such person as Plutarch than to say that there is one Plutarch who eats his children as soon as they are born."

Bishop James Pike tells of a young man coming to him with the news that he had become an atheist. Bishop Pike invited him to tell him about this God in whom he had come not to believe. As the young man described his rejected notion of God, Bishop Pike responded, "To tell you the truth, I don't believe in that kind of God either."

Imagine our "skeptic" responding to an angel's invitation to come and meet God. "But I've just told you that I'm not sure I believe in God."

"Come meet Him anyway."

Hear him say after the meeting, "This is the One I have loved and with whom I have longed to walk lo these many years!" (A heathen worshiping God ignorantly?)

Integrity rather than *institution* is the identifying mark of the invisible church, but this does not mean that institution is necessarily bad or irrelevant. Institution has negative connotations mainly in the sense of institutionalism, in which the means-value of structure or organization has taken priority over the end-value that it is supposed to serve. It is idolatrous to allow anything that is penultimate to assume the role that belongs to the Ultimate. The church as institution cannot be allowed to substitute itself for God. Nor can its aims, goals, and values be permitted to usurp God's aims, goals, and values.

As institutional Adventists, for example, we must never allow material evidences of success—such as numbers, buildings, and public acclaim—to become more important than the quality of our church's witness to the world.

I've sometimes wondered whether the finishing of the work in Islam, where cultural and social ties are so powerful and all-encompassing that entry of the Christian message has been virtually impossible (there is only one Adventist to every 50,000 people in the Middle East), may have to depend upon an indigenous movement within Islam. Might the members of such a movement preserve most of their cultural ties with Islam while capturing the essence of the gospel? Conceivably such might even consider themselves to be "true Muslims" much as Christians, following Paul's attitude in the New Testament, speak of "true Israel." Would we praise God for it? Would we even dare to foster it? Would we grant them institutional autonomy, or would we insist that these "true Muslims" sign on our Adventist institutional dotted line, including sending their tithes and offerings to the right place?

It is said that there was a time when all central Asia trembled in the balance—would it go toward Christ or toward Muhammad? In Marco Polo's time Kublai Khan sent a request to the Western world "for a hundred teachers and learned men, acquainted with the seven arts, able to enter into controversy and able to prove to idolaters and other kinds of folks that the law of Christ is best." But the Christian world was divided and filled with squabbles. After a delay of two years, two priests instead of 100 were sent, and they soon abandoned their expedition.

The Mongols were anything but impressed with Christianity and papal Rome. "Christianity so vitiated was not good enough for the Mongol mind," says Wells. They took Islam instead and swept across Asia with the Muslim sword spreading destruction and Islam wherever they went. As a result, the Middle East and much of central Asia became solidly Islamic. The church, carrying the name of Christ, failed. It was more interested in political power than in people, in controversy than in Christ.

The counterpart of the invisible church is the institutionalized church visible (visible to humans, that is). It is made up of those who publicly identify themselves as belonging to the general "body of Christ" through institutional symbols (such as crosses), names, labels, even with the label "Christian." There may be a variety of subdivisions of this entity (denominations) and a relative correspondence between their claim and the reality of their relation to Jesus Christ.

Their acknowledgment of membership could even be hypocritical and self-seeking. Quoting Isaiah 29:13, Jesus spoke of those who honor Him with their lips but whose hearts are far from Him (Matt. 15:8). He referred to people in His day whose public piety was designed to impress others and to win power and influence and said of them that "not everyone who says to me, 'Lord, Lord,' will enter the kingdom of heaven, but only he who does the will of my Father who is in heaven. Many will say to me on that day, 'Lord, Lord, did we not prophesy in your name, and in your name drive out demons and perform many miracles?' Then I will tell them plainly, 'I never knew you. Away from me, you evildoers!' " (Matt. 7:21-23).

External evidence is obviously not a sure indication of union with Christ. Some who claim membership in the visible church may, in fact, actually be separated from Him. Others may be His true followers, however, persons of integrity and compassion, living up to the light they have and thus also members of the invisible church. There is thus the possibility of two classes of members in the visible church—those, on the one hand, with dual citizenship, as it were, who are persons who manifest inner integrity while they make public their commitment to Christ, and, on the other, those who give lip service only, "whose hearts are far from Him." Both classes may superficially appear to honor the same cross and to wear the same label—at least until the harvest. (The wheat and the tares grow together until the harvest. Please refer to the diagram on p. 46.)

The point I wish to make is this, consideration of the visible church as a relatively united, viable, institutional structure, even though large and multifaceted, is not an irrelevant abstraction. As imperfect and fallible as it may be as it projects its witness, it still may function in some measure as the "body of Christ" on the earth, as a vehicle for the Word made flesh—at least until the end. It is not for anyone to judge one facet against another. The inner integrity of its members, or the lack of it, will become obvious on that day of testing when God shall reveal His own.

The term "visible church," used in so general a way, is intended as a counter to sectarian exclusivism. It recognizes that God is not bound to any single fragment of Christendom. God is nobody's private property, not even ours. As shocking as it may seem, God's name is not enrolled on the membership roster of the Seventh-day Adventist Church!

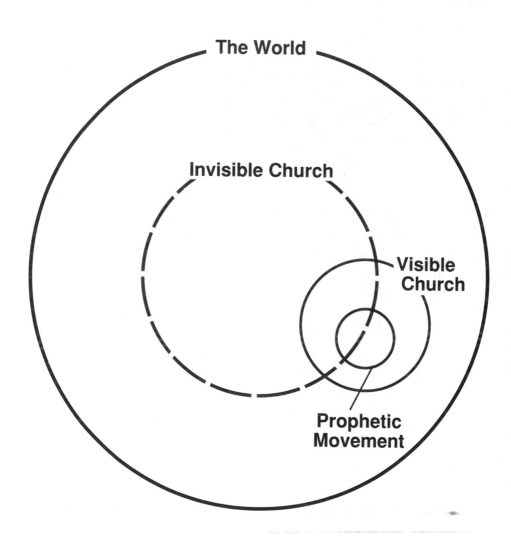

Abraham Lincoln gave good counsel in his reply to a deputation of Southerners who asked him on whose side God was in the great conflict. "My concern is not whether God is on my side; my great concern is to be on God's side."

Should not the church be most concerned about being part of that larger church, a church that includes as well as transcends all human structures and institutions and is united with the church in heaven?

The sense of universal communion that this suggests represents a maturation of world-view and a progression of understanding of the character of God. If God is our Father, then all men and women are our brothers and sisters whether or not they realize it or whether or not they wish to be. A maturing church will relish this truth. Unfortunately, it can also spell the end to the very quality that we noted as threatened in the developing Adventist crisis.

How can we speak of the church invisible and the church visible and of all men and women being our brothers and sisters and at the same time think of ourselves as "the people of God," "the remnant," "God's special church" having "the truth for our time"? The two notions seem at best to be anachronistic. At worst one is an apparent manifestation of hubris. This is especially so in light of the odds against our fulfilling the impossible task all by ourselves.

But if we lose the sense of specialness that such terms affirm, will we not have lost the very reason for our existence? Certainly we will have lost the crucible out of which is fired the energy that has brought us to where we are. As for few others, that sense is crucial to our very being. Lose it and we are essentially finished as a real force in the world.

Oh, there will probably always be an institutional Seventh-day Adventist Church. It is so well structured that a thousand years hence, if time should last, it will still be floating around somewhere. (General Conference president Reuben Figuhr used to say, "The machinery runs good," and he was right.) But without our historic sense of specialness, it will not make any pressing difference whether it continues or not.

Indeed, that is the key question of the present crisis. What difference does it make whether one is an Adventist, a Baptist, a Methodist, a Presbyterian, a Roman Catholic, or whatever? It is a good question. It is, in fact, a pivotal question, one we cannot avoid asking.

CHAPTER FOUR

A Prophetic Movement

DR. ARTHUR F. Glasser of Fuller Theological Seminary in Pasadena, California, recently wrote an article friendly to Adventists in *Ministry* magazine. He noted how he had come "to feel the struggles within a movement whose institutionalization processes of almost 150 years have eventuated in a troika of alternatives other evangelical bodies in our day also face. Shall it be a withdrawn, separatistic sect, just another accommodating church, or increasingly a prophesying remnant?" ("A Friendly Outsider Looks at Seventh-day Adventists," January 1989, p. 9).

In this reference to a "prophesying remnant" Dr. Glasser suggests the key to a resolution of one of the major tensions that threaten our identity. There is a third entity besides God's invisible and visible church that transcends yet belongs to both. As individual members of the church visible may, by reason of their integrity, also belong to the church invisible, just so members of this entity may be found among the "honest in heart" while sharing in institutional organization. They consciously maintain an open witness and make an obvious claim. They are visible, but they may also be honest as God reads their inner hearts.

The difference between this entity and the others is indicated by the word "prophesying." (I prefer Glasser's earlier term "movement" to his "remnant," and both his movement and remnant to "church," for reasons that will become apparent. The term "movement" emphasizes the spontaneous, unstructured vitality and inner fire of a group experiencing its first love. By contrast, a "church" is likely to be spending a disproportionate amount of its time and energy looking after its institutional business and fanning yesterday's embers. The term "movement" has been common coin for us for much of our history, and I use it here as an expression of hope that our first-love experience may be revived.) I submit that a partial resolution of the current tension may be found in categorizing the Seventh-day Adventist Church as a prophetic movement. (See diagram on p. 46.)

The term "prophetic" is crucial to what follows. Therefore it is important that we set forth precisely what is intended by its use in this context. We commonly infer from the word "prophet" a person who has the predictive gift. Accordingly, we assume that a prophet is one who foretells the future. "Prophetic" as an adjective refers to something touched by the gift.

The expression "prophetic movement" could, therefore, point to a movement preoccupied with making predictions, or even to one whose own coming has been predicted, that is, a movement that has itself been the object of prophecy. Or it could refer to a movement with a special interest in studying and interpreting predictive prophecy. All these could apply historically to the Seventh-day Adventist movement in one way or another. None, however, makes the point intended by the present use of the expression.

The prophet is here defined in terms of function and role. He or she is primarily a messenger—God's mouthpiece, God's voice to His people. The Old Testament prophets are classic examples. When God wanted to say something to His people, He called Moses, Isaiah, Jeremiah, Hosea, or Jonah. Each of these, and many others, were called to speak for Him in a particular time or place of need. But please note that they all were called to speak to God's people. They did not thereby become His people! The prophetic role is a service role, a role that is a means and not an end in itself.

Most of the prophets of old spoke as individuals, but there is also a role for collective, corporate prophets. A *people* can be called by God to function prophetically. Israel was the recipient of such a call. This is the underlying sense of the book bearing Jonah's name. Jonah, representing Israel in the story, is called to prophesy to God's people outside Israel. This was the larger meaning of Israel's call and covenant. They were established as "a kingdom of priests and an holy nation" with a mission to the world. They were called to be God's prophet to the world.

The book of Jonah relates the dramatic story of Israel's failure and a prophet's rebuke. Jonah (Israel) was unwilling to reach out to God's people in Gentile Nineveh. Instead of honoring their prophetic vocation, they had become merely an inward-turning, "special people."

See their sin in an ancient Jewish prayer. "O God, Thou has made us for Thyself; as for the rest of the nations they are but spittle." Each day such a pious Jew thanked God that he was not born "a leper, a woman, or a Gentile." (Let a "special people" in whatever age take note.) Specialness properly refers to role and function and to "present truth" rather than to divine favor. God is no respecter of persons whether as individuals or in groups.

The book of Jonah is one of the earliest and clearest biblical expressions of the universal Fatherhood of God and the brotherhood and sisterhood of all His children. The New Testament goes much further. "God so loved the *world*" (John 3:16, KJV). Jesus is "the true light that gives light to *every* man" (John 1:9) The disciples were to preach "in Jerusalem, and in all Judea, and Samaria, and to the *ends of the earth*" (Acts 1:8). God intended the good news of salvation to be preached "to every nation, tribe, language and people" (Rev. 14:6). "*Whosoever* is thirsty, let him come" (Rev. 22:17).

Since a prophetic movement's special message is its reason for being, it is important that we consider the prophetic genre at some length before we proceed to the main task of the present book. How does the prophetic gift work? Why and how does God use individual or collective prophets to accomplish His purposes in the world?

First, a word about prophets themselves and especially about the process by which they know the truth they are called to proclaim. We shall take as our point of departure a passage from *Testimonies*, volume 2, page 347. (The statement is repeated in a number of other places in the writings of Ellen White, suggesting that she considered it of some importance, which, philosophically, it truly is.) *"The brain nerves which communicate with the entire system are the only medium through which Heaven can communicate to man, and affect his inmost life."*

This is one solution to the ancient mind-body problem. (For a very long time people have wondered how the soma [body]—eyes, ears, touch, etc.—communicates with the psyche—soul or mind.) The psyche and the soma seem to be at such differing levels of reality that an impassable gap seems to separate them.

There are at least three points of view that form the presuppositions for thinking about the problem. One is a view in which the essential person is a soul—immortal, intangible, unchanging, beyond time and space—loosely and temporarily associated with a material body (a body that is the opposite of all these soul-qualities listed above). At death the immortal soul discards the body, which was nonessential in any case.

The philosopher Plato, who held this view, depicts Socrates as trying to console his disciples from whom he was about to depart. Crito asked Socrates, "But how shall we bury you?"

"Any way you like," said Socrates, "if I don't slip through your fingers."

A modern proponent of this view, Elisabeth Kübler-Ross, says
> Death is simply a shedding of the physical body like a
> butterfly coming out of a cocoon. It is a transition into a
> higher state of consciousness, where you continue to

perceive, to understand, to laugh, to be able to grow, and the only thing you lose is something you don't need anymore, and that is your physical body. It's like putting away your winter coat when spring comes and you know that the coat is too shabby and you don't want to wear it anymore ("Death Does Not Exist," *The Journal of Holistic Health*, 1977, p. 63).

Augustine, and others who were influenced by Plato's dualism, believed on such grounds that God (who is spirit) speaks to humans soul to soul with no need to go through the body. Truth is revealed as an inner light: "Spiritual things are spiritually discerned." We know the truth, not as a rational process, but from intuitions "from the pit of our mystical stomach" as it were. (Gut reaction?)

Opposed to this psychic reduction is a fairly contemporary, almost mechanical, somatic reduction (to their credit, now being revised by many neurophysiologists), in which knowing can be reduced to neurons and central nervous system chemistry, transmitter substances, etc., which are complicated, indeed, but not essentially mysterious.

Some revisionist neurophysiologists are, fortunately, now coming to opt, by and large, for a third view, in which soul and body, psyche and soma, are seen as dimensions of a unitary whole, a whole that is greater than the sum of its neurological processes and parts.

Ellen White's statement about the "brain-nerves" communicating with the entire system is consistent with her wholistic understanding of human nature. The human body counts. We have no intelligent existence apart from it, but we cannot be reduced to it. There is more. There is also mind and reason and feeling—knowing with the heart. Mind and body interact. Observe how this comes across in the following:

Whatever injures the health not only lessens physical vigor, but tends to weaken the mental and moral powers.

Indulgence in any unhealthful practice makes it more difficult for one to discriminate between right and wrong, and hence more difficult to resist evil. It increases the danger of failure and defeat (Ellen G. White, *The Ministry of Healing*, p. 128).

The relation that exists between the mind and the body is very intimate. When one is affected, the other sympathizes. The condition of the mind affects the health to a far greater degree than many realize. Many of the diseases from which men suffer are the result of mental depression. Grief, anxiety, discontent, remorse, guilt, distrust, all tend to break down the life forces and to invite decay and death (*ibid.*, p. 241).

More apropos to our present discussion are the even more numerous wholistic statements from the pen of Ellen White that associate perception with character and past experience. Here are some examples:

Every impure thought defiles the soul, impairs the moral sense, and tends to obliterate the impressions of the Holy Spirit. It dims the spiritual vision so men cannot behold God (*The Desire of Ages*, p. 302).

Selfishness prevents us from beholding God. The self-seeking spirit judges of God as altogether such a one as itself. Until we renounce this we cannot understand Him who is love (*ibid.*).

Let none suppose that they can live a life of selfishness, and then, having served their own interests, enter into the joy of their Lord. In the joy of unselfish love they could not participate. They would not be fitted for the heavenly courts. They could not appreciate the pure atmosphere of love that pervades heaven. . . . To their minds the science of heaven would be an enigma

(*Christ's Object Lessons*, pp. 364, 365).

Ellen White said of Satan:

> That the Son of God should come to this earth as a
> man filled him with amazement and with apprehension.
> He could not fathom the mystery of this great sacrifice.
> His selfish soul could not understand such love for the
> deceived race (*The Desire of Ages*, p. 115).

These statements remind us that each of us sees things not as *they* are but as *we* are. Each of us perceives things in a paradigm of meaning that is formed by a combination of what we have done or experienced (recalled or otherwise), our characters, our worldview, and our consciousness of ourselves. This paradigm forms a filter through which all new experience must pass. This means that all our perceptions of reality are in a measure skewed—and skewed for some of us more than for others—by the kind of people we are.

Paradigms are dynamic. New experience modifies them. To illustrate, one's conception of God may be conditioned either negatively or positively by experiences with abusing or nurturing parents. Fortunately, bad parenting may often be compensated for by other parent-surrogates whom the child may later encounter. Experiencing love can go a long way toward making love comprehensible, and this is mainly what the Christian community is all about. Love is discovered in a situation of love. This is surely the meaning of the following:

> Looking unto Jesus we obtain brighter and more
> distinct views of God, and by beholding we become
> changed. Goodness, love for our fellow men, becomes
> our natural instinct. We develop a character which is the
> counterpart of the divine character. Growing into His
> likeness, we enlarge our capacity for knowing God
> (*Christ's Object Lessons*, p. 355).

And, I might add, it modifies our manner of "knowing" everything else.

The process whereby our paradigm of meaning is modified is only relatively under our conscious control. Most of the events that affect us just "happen." Insofar as we have the capacity to choose our experiences, however, including those that God brings within the ranges of our freedom, we are given a measure of control over, and accountability for, the process. We are not required to experience all the things that take place in our world (including in our homes—or what are those channel-changing and off buttons for?). We may choose to, or not to, attend. We are not at the mercy of all the "happenings" in our lives.

The role of freedom in all this, although sometimes minimal, is pivotal. (We shall be exploring freedom more fully in a later context.) Freedom is the basis for our earlier observation that truth is progressive. Since our perception of reality—our paradigm of meaning—is conditioned by such qualities as our character, if God were to imprint meaning upon our minds directly, bypassing the "brain-nerves" and their ordinary knowing processes, this would mean that He could also simply superimpose upon us the character foundation for knowing the truth. Indeed, such a superimposition might be a logical necessity, in which case character would lose its moral relevance, just as the sounds from a taperecording do not render the recorder morally responsible.

But God values human freedom. It is a major part of what is meant by God's image in mankind. Our freedom to choose—as over against being merely imprinted with complex behavioral patterns—is fundamental to the formation of our character. Thus, to be consistent He has to let us in on the action, often requiring us to find our own way, allowing us not only to "see" but to interpret what we see—as we perceive it.

God's revelation to us is thus essentially an educative process. (Eighteenth-century German philosopher/theologian G. Lessing wrote about this in terms of "the education of the human race.") It

takes time, indeed the whole of human history, to get the full story
told, because God values human freedom. We must, with His help,
climb the ladder of understanding round by round. Enlisting His help
may include attending to the tasks that He has given us to perform in
the world.

> God created man that every faculty might be the
> faculty of the divine mind; and He is ever seeking to bring
> the human mind into association with the divine. He
> offers us the privilege of cooperation with Christ in
> revealing His grace to the world, that we may receive
> increased knowledge of heavenly things (*ibid.*).

The point has been labored because the key passage above, "The
brain nerves . . . are the only medium through which Heaven can
communicate to man, and affect his inmost life," is nonspecific. It
appears to apply to all of us. And this must include prophets. The
prophetic call does not literally translate its recipient, at least during
this life, to the realms of glory. Prophets are also human beings, and
they too must view reality through paradigmatic filters. Their perceptions, too, are conditioned by culture, character, and backgrounds of
experience. Prophets, as well as the rest of us, see things not as things
are, but as *they themselves* are.

Just how, then, do the prophets differ? The main differences have
not so much to do with the prophets as with the actions of God. There
are three chief distinctions.

1. Since individual paradigms differ one from another (certainly
in their transparency to reality), some filters permit perceptions less
skewed by character and experience than others. The prophets are
chosen as vehicles for special truth, not because their comprehension
and transmission would be flawless, but because they are the best
vehicle. Theirs is the most transparent paradigm, and they are
available (and willing) at the moment of need. If God wants truth
ultimately to prevail, He cannot call just anyone off the street to be a

prophet. Prophets are chosen, selected, set apart—for good reasons. They are decent people, even though relatively flawed by their humanity.

2. The prophets are given a voice. There is no point in calling prophets to whom nobody listens. Prophets must command attention. Those to whom they are sent must see in them someone special, someone different from the ordinary. This extraordinary quality will usually be accommodated to cultural conditions and expectations. John the Baptist looked like a prophet to the Jews of the first century. He ate like a prophet, dressed like a prophet, and spoke like a prophet. That camel's hair coat! They couldn't be sure it wasn't Elijah himself returned from heaven. They knew, of course, of Malachi's prediction (Mal. 4:5).

Some prophets were called in extraordinary ways (Moses and the burning bush), and they were asked to do unusual things (Jeremiah wore an ox-yoke around his neck; Ezekiel lay on his left side for 390 days). Ellen White's condition in vision in the early days of her ministry powerfully influenced the establishment of her prophetic role. The observation that she didn't breathe was awesome. Later, the fruits of her labors—her books, counsel, etc.—would provide the necessary assurance. Sometimes it was prophetic metaphor, sometimes it was hyperbole that proved persuasive. Prophets often tended to overstate for effect. They shouted to be heard. (That's one of the differences between prophets and systematic theologians.)

3. Having selected and called the prophets because of the relative transparency of their paradigmatic filters, and having provided them with a platform to stand on (the prophetic roles), God then gave special communications. Sometimes the messages came in an extraordinary manner, such as in visions or dreams. Most of the time they came in rather ordinary ways, such as thoughts, impressions, and intuitions, which were perceived by the prophet as the prompting of the Spirit. (Ellen White apparently often "heard" the voice of God

speaking to her as she read books in her library. A person who had spent a lifetime as God's messenger would surely develop unusual sensitivity to such intuitions and might even quite understandably employ, at times, the very words of the authors through which they were presented to her mind—with or without quotation marks.)

The reasons for discussing the prophetic call and work to such an extent have to do with the fact that many of the things that we have said about prophets equally apply to a prophetic movement. Certainly God's call and the establishing of the role so apply. (John the Baptist as the Elijah-messenger of his day has much to say to the bearers of the Elijah message of today.) The extraordinary manifestations, the visions, dreams, etc., by which the prophets are given a role may be less obvious in the case of the corporate prophet. The special messages may come in more ordinary ways, perhaps involving something more like study and learning. Groups do not ordinarily experience visions, etc. The presence and guidance of a gifted individual, Ellen White, has helped mightily to provide the special communications for the Adventist prophetic movement.

The main similarity between the prophet and the prophetic movement is this: The prophetic call in both cases is founded on message. The prophets' entire reason for being as prophets has to do with what they have to say. Without a message prophets are just like everybody else. No message, no prophet. It's that simple. And so with prophetic movements. The crisis facing the Adventist prophetic movement can be met only by a rediscovery of and dedication to what God has commissioned this people to say in the world. *Note*

There are many other things we can and must do in the world simply as Christians—along with our fellow Christians in the visible church. We share a great deal with them, including most of our 27 fundamental beliefs. But our prophetic role involves something more. It is clarity about this "something more" that will enable this people to retain its vitality and sense of vocation. Without our special message, we are just another part of the visible church, in which case it makes little difference whether we are Adventists, Baptists, Methodists, Presbyterians, Roman Catholics, or whatever—providing that we are Christians.

CHAPTER FIVE

A Voice in the Wilderness

C RITICS tend to dismiss the sense of mission early associated in Adventism with such terms as "people of God," "remnant," and "true church" as a sectarian aberration based on ignorance, if not frank delusion or personality disorder. The truth may be quite the opposite, however, providing that the reality those terms express is truly not illusory, that we really do have something to say.

It sometimes happens that mission succumbs to education. Pushing the horizons back too far and too fast can stress the meaning-paradigms of individuals to beyond what they can easily assimilate. But usually the more we know, the more inclusive our worldview, the more persons we encounter, and the deeper and more intimate that encounter, the less egocentric and more realistic our perceptions of reality may become.

What this means is that as a prophetic movement grows in understanding and becomes ever more mature in its witness, it may become more committed to (albeit less exclusive about) its prophetic mission. It may come increasingly to appreciate Jesus' words to Peter when asked about the future role of "the disciple whom Jesus loved," John.

"Lord, what about him?" Peter asked.

"Jesus answered, 'If I want him to remain alive until I return, what is that to you? You must follow me' " (John 21:21, 22).

Are there or have there ever been other "prophets"? That is possible. It may even be probable. But what is that to us? Each prophet has his or her own call, his or her own message to bear. The Adventist message is ours. It is timely, and it is special. If others also contribute to the finishing of the work on the earth, thanks be to God! After all, it is God's work, and the Almighty is nobody's exclusive possession.

The special sense of mission that such words convey is vulnerable, however. It is easily overwhelmed by uncertainty about the true nature of that mission. This is a point of some importance, providing the key to what we shall attempt to accomplish in the remaining chapters.

We noted earlier that true prophets derive their role-value and their reason for being from what they have to say. No true prophet ever comes running up after the battle, gasping breathlessly, "I saw great confusion . . . , but I don't know what it was" (2 Sam. 18:29). Again, no message; no prophet.

A recapturing of the vitalizing energy of our movement's early years depends upon our being able to see again—in our time—the essence of what seemed so clear in theirs. (By "essence" we mean that which defines—the central core of the matter, as over against elements that are incidental, peripheral, or unimportant. The essentials of a set of ideas or propositions remain constant, while the incidental manner of their expression may vary, even fairly radically, from time to time and place to place. It should not surprise us to find fundamental beliefs of one prophetic generation being expressed in quite different language and thought forms from another. This may be threatening, of course, to individuals who are unclear about the essentials.)

As we begin our quest for the essentials of the Seventh-day Adventist message, one thing we should not expect is absolute novelty. This, too, might disturb some. How can we talk of "specialness" when we find others singing the same tune, or at least joining in on the chorus? However, is not this precisely what we should expect if truth is progressive? The God of progressive truth would not wait until the end to spring total surprises on us. Someone has said, "Ideas are never immaculately conceived." That is, they always have a past. L. E. Froom has reminded us of this truism in his exhaustive *Prophetic Faith of Our Fathers*. All "new light" presupposes previous light. Everything, almost, that Adventists have to say has been said before by someone else, even if only in a partial and preliminary mode. Adventism resonates to something written by Howard Snyder about John Wesley.

> According to some critics, John Wesley never had an original idea in his life. He just borrowed from others. Even if true, this would hardly solve the riddle of Wesley. His genius and originality lay precisely in his borrowing, adapting, and combining diverse elements into a synthesis more dynamic than the sum of its parts (*The Radical Wesley*, p. 143).

It was the way things were put together that constituted Wesley's originality. (Snyder's statement about Wesley could be applied equally to Ellen White. Given the loss of confidence experienced by many Adventists over the "borrowing issue," this is something worth thinking about.) We speak of the Wesleyan synthesis. So with the Adventist movement. God intended that the truth progressively unfolding during the centuries should finally all come together at the end of time. (The Adventist synthesis?)

Let us see, now, if we can justify the prophetic claim to specialness. First, though not total, there is a measure of uniqueness. (I realize that one can be no more a little bit unique than one can be a little bit pregnant. What I wish to convey here is that in the midst of sameness there can be elements of difference.) No other denomination that I know of claims as its own the three-angels' message of

Revelation 14. (Following Ellen White, I consider the three to be one united message. Cf. *Testimonies*, vol. 6, p. 17 and *Selected Messages*, book 2, p. 116.)

Those who deliver it are identified as "saints." "This calls for patient endurance on the part of the *saints* who obey God's commandments and remain faithful to Jesus" (Rev. 14:12). Now, "saint" is a very interesting word. Ordinarily we use the term as indicating superlative goodness. For me to speak of my "sainted mother" means that I consider her to be a very good woman. Rudolph Otto (see *The Idea of the Holy*, pp. 5-7) points out that there is a cluster of terms, such as "holy," "hallowed," "sacred," "sanctified," "saintly," that have a double layer of meaning. They can mean "good," as above, but this ethical meaning was not the original meaning and never the whole meaning of such terms.

Otto says that there is an overplus of meaning in such words that goes beyond the ethical to something more. This overplus is what we would be thinking of when we say "set apart" or "special." Otto uses the term "numinous." The Sabbath day when it was hallowed did not become a "good" day. It became a "special" day—sanctified, set apart by God. Being a saint in a prophetic movement does not carry an intimation of perfection as much as it represents a discovery of one's special place in the scheme of things. (Though, of course, being saintly couldn't hurt either. Saints also "obey God's commandments.")

Two components constitute the three-angels' message, one positive and the other negative. The positive message is proclaimed by the first angel, and the negative message is proclaimed by the second and third. The essence of the message is contained in the words of the first angel. The second and third proclamations, in effect, underscore the consummate tragedy of not attending to what the first angel had to say.

I say this despite the fact that Adventists have traditionally tended to emphasize numbers two and three, being certain to interpret the troublesome "forever and ever" in such a way as to keep the text consistent with the general biblical teaching regarding the state of the dead. A statement by the prophet at the height of her powers, in one of her defenses of the position she took in connection with the 1888 conference in Minneapolis, clearly so identifies it. In this statement she identifies the third angel's message with the gospel, the good news. (Note how three angels' messages had become the three-angels' message [*Testimonies*, vol. 6, p. 17], and now the third angel's message—all synonyms.) The article was first published in the *Review and Herald*, April 1, 1890 (later reproduced in *Selected Messages*, book 1, p. 372). I quote at some length in order to capture her spirit more effectively.

> Some of our brethren have expressed fears that we shall dwell too much upon the subject of justification by faith, but I hope and pray that none will be needlessly alarmed; for there is no danger in presenting this doctrine as it is set forth in the Scriptures. If there had not been a remissness in the past to properly instruct the people of God, there would not now be a necessity of calling special attention to it. . . . The exceeding great and precious promises given us in the Holy Scriptures have been lost sight of to a great extent, just as the enemy of all righteousness designed that they should be. He has cast his own dark shadow between us and our God, that we may not see the true character of God. The Lord has proclaimed Himself to be "merciful and gracious, long-suffering, and abundant in goodness and truth."
>
> Several have written to me, inquiring if the message of justification by faith is the third angel's message, and I have answered, "It is the third angel's message in

verity" (Ellen G. White, *Selected Messages*, book 1, p. 372).

This passage is consistent with a reference to the final message in Ellen White's *Christ's Object Lessons*.

It is the darkness of misapprehension of God that is enshrouding the world. Men are losing their knowledge of His character. It has been misunderstood and misinterpreted. *At this time* a message from God is to be proclaimed, a message illuminating in its influence and saving in its power. His character is to be made known. Into the darkness of the world is to be shed the light of His glory, the light of His goodness, mercy, and truth (p. 415; italics supplied).

The final synthesis of truth is, in a phrase, the truth about God. But remember that this is a synthesis. Several aspects of the truth about God come together in that essential theme of the first angel: gospel, judgment, Creator. We shall need to look at these individually and collectively, beginning with what must certainly be the foremost in importance.

The truth about God is, above all else, that He is Creator. "Worship him who made the heavens, the earth, the sea and the springs of water" (Rev. 14:7). That God is the Creator is the most important thing anyone can say about Him. The fallout from that statement runs for miles and miles—literally, for light-years and light-years—and never has it been more important to keep our language and thought forms up-to-date.

Many among us have little notion of the implications of "God is Creator." A lady is reported to have asked a famous, believing astronomer at the conclusion of his lecture on the vastness and grandeur of the universe how anyone could believe in God given what he had just told them. He responded, "It all depends on the size of the God you worship, madam." The lady's question shared something of what the great Laplace, framer of universal evolution, said in a similar situation: "I have no need of that hypothesis."

In the introduction to his popular book *Your God Is Too Small*, Bible translator J. B. Phillips says (and he could be addressing the Adventist crisis):

> The trouble with many people today is that they have not found a God big enough for modern needs. While their experience of life has grown in a score of directions, and their mental horizons have been expanded to the point of bewilderment by world events and by scientific discoveries, their ideas of God have remained largely static. It is obviously impossible for an adult to worship the conception of God that exists in the mind of a child of Sunday-school age, unless he is prepared to deny his own experience of life. If, by a great effort of will, he does do this, he will always be secretly afraid lest some new truth may expose the juvenility of his faith. And it will always be by such an effort that he either worships or serves a God who is really too small to command his adult loyalty and cooperation.

> It often appears to those outside the churches that this is precisely the attitude of Christian people. If they are not strenuously defending an outgrown conception of God, then they are cherishing a hothouse God who could only exist between the pages of the Bible or inside the four walls of a church. Therefore to join in with the worship of a church would be to become a party to a piece of mass-hypocrisy and to buy a sense of security at the price of the sense of truth, and many men of goodwill will not consent to such a transaction (pp. v, vi).

Phillips writes of a number of conceptions of God that are too small to correspond to the awesome reality: God as a resident policeman; God as a Freudian, parental hangover; God in a private box; etc. One likely to commend itself to the thoughtful mind is God as a managing director, the thought being that as an owner of a small business one is likely to know a great deal about his employees and their families. The larger the business and the greater the number of employees he has working for him, the less he will know about them, until as the managing director of a large corporation with hundreds or thousands under him, he will know next to nothing—perhaps only the names of a few key department heads. The greater the responsibilities, the more numerous the individuals involved, and the wider the scope of his concerns, as managing director the less he will know about the individual lives he has under his purview.

Thornton Wilder makes the same point in his three-act play *Our Town*, in which he gives the address of one of his characters as

Jane Crowfoot

The Crowfoot farm

Grover's Corners

Sutton County

New Hampshire

United States of America

Continent of North America

Western Hemisphere

The Earth

The Solar System

The Universe

The Mind of God

As far as I can see, the only things Thornton Wilder left out are Jane Crowfoot's zip code and the Milky Way Galaxy. But note, please, where the mind of God is, away out at the most distant of a series of concentric circles. He is remote and far, far away. That's the Deist's error, of course, the "Absentee Landlord" God who started things going and then left them to run all by themselves.

If one's intellectual horizons are pushed back far enough, it is an easy error to make. It would take 20 billion light-years, that is, *20 billion years*, traveling at 186,000 miles per second (that's seven times around the earth before one can take two steps) to travel from one edge of the known universe to the other. And there are more than 100 billion galaxies or island universes out there, each made up of hundreds of billions of stars. (Our Milky Way Galaxy alone has 300 billion stars in it.)

Taken altogether, there are more than a hundred-thousand-million-billion stars in the universe—and planets, some of them possibly inhabited. Who knows? Recently astronomers thought they had finally found evidence of a distant planet, an extremely difficult accomplishment given the fact that planets are not usually known to be sources of light. This supposed planet probably could not sustain life as we know it because of the nature of its sun. Later it was discovered that the findings were in error. But how many are there really out there? If we assumed only one planet for every 10 billion suns, we would still have about 10 billion planets. Many scientists think that one planet to every 10 billion suns is too small by a factor of a million, at least, in which case the universe would contain something like 10 quadrillion (one followed by 16 zeros) planets capable of supporting life.

If we add to this the statements of Jesus that all the hairs on our heads are numbered and that no sparrow falls without the Father's notice (hairs on the heads of all those planetary dwellers—and their sparrows, too?), God has a lot on His mind, surely too much to know that my rent isn't paid, my wife is ill, and my child needs shoes.

And there's the rub with the managing director picture of God.

Ah, but there is another side to that picture. Nothing said about God in the Bible is clearer than that He is Creator of everything that is, and not only Creator but Sustainer, "sustaining all things by his powerful word" (Heb. 1:3).

Ellen White tells us, "In the creation of the earth, God was not indebted to preexisting matter" (*The Ministry of Healing*, p. 414). Ever since $E = mc^2$ this has also meant that God was not dependent upon previously existing energy. (Matter and energy are now seen as interchangeable.) No material or energy would even exist apart from God's sustaining power.

This means that God is "in touch" with His entire universe, with every subatomic particle, as well as with the massive galactic structures of the heavens. Nothing happens in His universe but it, in some way, happens to Him.

Now, wait a minute, you say. When we spoke of the hairs on all those planetary heads, and the sparrows, we proposed that God has a lot on His mind. Now we see that Jane Crowfoot's final address was even more inclusive than we dreamed. See how this comes through in a pair of passages in Ellen White's writings:

> Few give thought to the suffering that sin has caused our Creator. All heaven suffered in Christ's agony; but that suffering did not begin or end with His manifestation in humanity. The cross is a revelation to our dull senses of the pain that, from its very inception, sin has brought to the heart of God. . . . Our world is a vast lazar house, a scene of misery that we dare not allow even our thoughts to dwell upon. Did we realize it as it is, the burden would be too terrible. Yet God feels it all (Ellen G. White, *Education*, pp. 263, 264).

> From the stars that in their trackless courses through space follow from age to age their appointed path, down to the minutest atom, the things of nature obey the Creator's will. And God cares for everything and sustains everything that He has created. He who upholds the unnumbered worlds throughout immensity, at the same time cares for the wants of the little brown sparrow that

sings its humble song without fear. When men go forth to their daily toil, as when they engage in prayer, when they lie down at night, and when they rise in the morning, when the rich man feasts in his palace, or when the poor man gathers his children about the scanty board, each is tenderly watched by the heavenly Father. No tears are shed that God does not notice. There is no smile that He does not mark (Ellen G. White, *Steps to Christ*, p. 86).

And there's the managing director again. How can it be? With so much on His mind, how can God know about *my* troubles? The answer to that question is hinted at by a human analogy, as is so much of the truth about God. Every awake person is constantly bombarded by a flood of sensations. I saw the figure once of 12 million sense impressions per minute. Twelve million sense impressions per minute would be so totally inundating as to render all rational thought impossible were it not for the capacity of the mind to attend to and concentrate on only a minute fraction of the total at any one time, and this is to some extent selective, and therefore there are freedom and responsibility.

And so with God. God is big enough to be in touch with His entire universe without losing His ability to be selective about me. Galileo once said, "The sun, with all those planets revolving around it and dependent on it, can still ripen a bunch of grapes as if it had nothing else in the universe to do."

The point of all this is that as a prophetic movement tries to sort out its special message, it had better be prepared to contemplate a vastly more exalted reality paradigm than our fathers BQP (before quantum physics) knew, and to find ways of coming to terms with it—if it is to be taken seriously. (Renowned Jewish scholar and thinker Abraham Joshua Heschel once said to me, "You Adventists have a wonderful message, but you must learn to present it with greater sophistication so that people will take you seriously." And he was right, if we recognize that sophistication and simplicity are not necessarily antonyms.) The Adventist synthesis is about a God who is big enough to create and sustain the universe but not so small as to become lost in it.

CHAPTER SIX

God Is Creator

TO SAY that God is Creator, with all that implies, is the most important thing any prophetic movement can say about Him. The call to "worship him who made the heavens, the earth, the sea and the springs of water" (Rev. 14:7) lies at the very foundation of the Adventist synthesis. It touches and underscores every aspect of God's final message to the world. It is important, therefore, here at the beginning of our quest for the essence of the prophetic movement's message that we explore the ramifications of that statement.

Unfortunately, to speak of creation is usually an invitation to awaken tensions that have divided Fundamentalist, conservative, and liberal church members for most of the Christian church's existence. The conflict is primarily over how to relate reason and observation to revelation. How shall we understand the Bible? Are the Genesis accounts to be regarded as straightforward, literal history, or are they examples of the following?

The Lord speaks to human beings in imperfect speech, in order that the degenerate senses, the dull, earthly perception, of earthly beings may comprehend His words. Thus is shown God's condescension. He meets fallen human beings where they are. The Bible, perfect as it is in its simplicity, does not answer to the great ideas of God, for infinite ideas cannot be perfectly embodied in finite vehicles of thought (*Selected Messages*, book 1, p. 22).

A trivial analogy. Some years ago I was musing alone down by the corral where we kept our two quarter horses. Near the corral was a large anthill teeming with red ants. I thought to myself, *How would a human go about communicating with creatures at that level?* I was aware, of course, of the scientific attempts to communicate with higher animals such as dolphins, but with ants? They seemed oblivious of my presence.

I stamped my foot near the anthill. They seemed to scurry about more rapidly. I fantasized that one of them said to another, "Say, that was a sharp one. I wonder what its reading on the Richter scale was?"

I went to the tack room and picked up a handful of grain mixed with molasses. I dropped the grain into the opening at the top of the anthill. Say, did they scurry then! Again I fantasized one of them saying, "What luck! What a great summer we've had!"

Still they remained totally unaware of my nearness or my interest in them.

Laying aside triviality, the only way to communicate with ants is to become an ant oneself, to strew pheromones around, rub antennae, or whatever ants do when they "talk" (I understand that some ants have small vibratory organs by which they signal each other), and that's what the Incarnation was all about. "The Word was made flesh and dwelt among us" (John 1:14, KJV). But remember, if one becomes an ant to talk to ants, the ants will still hear as ants—in ant paradigms. Is the Word of God conditioned by human paradigms? Probably, although it is not reducible to them. As in the ant analogy, Someone is out there trying to reach us, trying again and again.

(A number of our natural scientists are having difficulty with Genesis as literal history. Some are going the way of most evangelicals [not the radical verbal-inspiration Fundamentalists], who, having no Sabbath problems, are coming to think in terms of progressive creation and theistic evolution. I would only warn such that to attribute the salient features of the theory of evolution to God is to come up with the wrong kind of God! The God of the evolutionary hypothesis, as it is commonly understood, would be Nietzsche's god, not the Father of Jesus Christ. More on this later.)

The essential core of the call to worship the Creator has not so much to do with history or with the nature of a process (which we probably wouldn't understand in any case) as it has to do with the nature of reality. The details of what happened may have to wait for eternity, but there are some things we can know even now. Among these is that just as God is one ("Hear, O Israel: The Lord our God, the Lord is one" [Deut. 6:4] and is Creator of everything that is, so His creation is one. God created a uni-verse and not a multi-verse. See how this comes through in one of Ellen White's more heuristic statements. (Mark this passage for future reference.)

> In dwelling upon the laws of matter and the laws of nature, many lose sight of, if they do not deny, the continual and direct agency of God. They convey the idea that nature acts independently of God, having in and of itself its own limits and its own powers wherewith to work. In their minds there is a marked distinction between the natural and the supernatural. The natural is ascribed to ordinary causes, unconnected with the power of God. . . . This is false science; there is nothing in the Word of God to sustain it. God does not annul His laws, but He is continually working through them, using them as His instruments. They are not self-working. . . . Nature in her work testifies of the intelligent presence and active agency of a Being who moves in all His works according to His will. It is not by an original power inherent in nature that year by year the earth yields its bounties and continues its march around the sun. The hand of infinite

power is perpetually at work guiding this planet. It is God's power momentarily exercised that keeps it in position in its rotation.

The God of heaven is constantly at work. It is by His power that vegetation is caused to flourish, that every leaf appears and every flower blooms. Every drop of rain or flake of snow, every spire of grass, every leaf and flower and shrub, testifies of God. . . . The mechanism of the human body can not be fully understood; it presents mysteries that baffle the most intelligent. It is not as the result of a mechanism, which, once set in motion, continues its work, that the pulse beats and breath follows breath. In God we live and move and have our being. Every breath, every throb of the heart, is a continual evidence of the power of an ever-present God.

It is God that causes the sun to rise in the heavens. [As G. K. Chesterton once put it: "The only reason the sun gets up in the morning is because God says, 'All right, do it again.' "] He opens the windows of heaven and gives rain. He causes the grass to grow upon the mountains (*Testimonies*, vol. 8, pp. 259, 260).

There are a number of obvious implications of this profound statement. Never was monotheism stated in more radical terms. First, we must explore what it might mean to worship so intimate yet so exalted a Being.

Webster defines worship in terms of reverence, veneration, respect, admiration, and devotion. For creatures to worship their Creator is to hold these attitudes and feelings toward this Ultimate Ground of their being, to give to God the highest priority in all their valuing and acting, to put God first in all that they want and do. Professor Paul Tillich defined religion as that which concerns one ultimately. True worship is to give to the Creator that position of ultimacy. The three-angels' message, which begins with a call to worship, ends by identifying those who respond to the call as those who "obey God's commandments" (Rev. 14:12). The highest act of worship is willing obedience.

To worship God is to choose to live in harmony with the Creator's will, to fit willingly into the pattern or niche designed in and for us by the Creator and Sustainer of all things. To disobey the commandments is to choose to thwart the Creator's design and purpose. Obedience and disobedience both presuppose the gift of intelligence and freedom.

Human beings are the only earthly creatures who can consciously reject their Creator and thus their own creatureliness. We are also the only earthly creatures in which that rejection makes any real difference, because only we are free. The monotheistic premise, stated so colorfully in the quotation above and depicting God's ultimate role in the scheme of things, implies that to disobey God is to act against one's own being. To sin against God is to sin against one's true self, and vice versa. They are but two sides of one coin.

Moral theologians sometimes draw a distinction between natural and moral law. According to the monotheistic premise, both participate in the universal orderliness that makes up the kingdom of God. One emphasizes things and processes, the other, personal and interpersonal relationships, but both are the law of God. Neither can be violated with impunity. Information about both, whether derived from investigation or revelation, constitutes God's grace guiding us to self-fulfillment. Such grace is rejected at one's peril. Those who discover and accept this truth are those who have come to know with the psalmist, "Great peace have they who love your law, and nothing can make them stumble" (Ps. 119:165).

Appreciation for God's gracious revelation of His law as the way to true self-fulfillment has from the very beginning been essential to this movement's prophetic message. This is especially the case with His having chosen a moment of time, the Sabbath of the fourth commandment, to remind us of His creative sovereignty over all time.

The Sabbath provides an occasion to underscore the synthetic nature of the message. In the Adventist synthesis the parts all come together in a whole that is greater than the sum total of all the parts.

(Review Snyder's remarks on Wesley on p. 63.) The parts also support and reinforce each other in the synthesis. The fourth commandment reinforces the entire law in its perpetuity, as we shall see.

The Sabbath also provides an opportunity to illustrate something we noted earlier about a movement's growth and development, about discovering "new light" while maintaining continuity with former truths, about a tree continuing its connection with its roots without becoming root-bound.

For most of the movement's history, emphasis has been placed on establishing the perpetuity of God's ten-commandment law, including and especially the fourth commandment. We have exposed the biblical foundations for Sabbathkeeping, traced its history, noted the papal changes, and outlined the Sabbath's role in the final polarization of the remnant and Babylon, resulting in a conflict between those who bear the seal of God (the Sabbath) and those who receive the mark of the beast (Sunday). A major motivation for our conservative treatment of the Genesis account of Creation has been our compulsion to preserve the Sabbath and its presupposing six-day Creation.

Unfortunately, this emphasis has failed to ensure Sabbathkeeping in the strictest sense. Many Adventists have come to think of Sabbathkeeping much as other Christians think of keeping Sunday, a time for play and relaxation and for "lay activities," such as sleep. (Some Adventist "old-timers" are having trouble with a vision of the young amusing themselves playing ball, waterskiing, and the like on Sabbath afternoon—with the apparent sanction of their elders who have their own equivalents. And some of them are wondering whether the Sabbath may be slipping through Adventist fingers.)

But the viability of the Sabbath does not depend upon earth-history, biblical apologetics, or historical church backgrounds—as important as these may have been in establishing its factual reality. Having established its historicity beyond question, Seventh-day Adventists should now be concentrating on the meaning of the Sabbath and its role in what God is doing in the world. Proper Sabbathkeeping is not so simple as legalistic conformity to all the Ten Commandments.

In the Bible the Sabbath is referred to as a sign. "You must observe my Sabbaths. This will be a sign between me and you for the generations to come, so you may know that I am the Lord, who makes you holy" (Ex. 31:13). (The NIV footnote to this text gives an alternate rendering, "Or who sanctifies you; or who sets you apart as holy." Recall our earlier observations about "saints," as in "patience of the saints" in Revelation 14:12 [KJV].) It seems appropriate that the Sabbath should be the mark of a "set-apart" people in whatever age. "It will be a sign between me and the Israelites forever" (Ex. 31:17) can apply to spiritual as well as to literal Israel. (Ezekiel 20:13, 20 reiterates what is said in Exodus 31.)

Some theologians make a useful distinction between "sign" and "symbol." The two terms are alike in some ways, notably in their pointing function. Both gain their value because they refer to and stand for something else. They also share in their universality. Almost any entity—abstract or concrete, object or action, thing or person— can function as a sign or symbol. Examples are endless. They differ mainly in that signs are arbitrary. Signs bear no necessary relation to that to which they point. They are assigned to them. The so-called symbols of mathematics or given names in our society are good examples. X equals the unknown by convention. Z or Y could do quite as well. Given names are usually unconsciously derived from someone prominent in the news or from a favored relative perhaps. (In Bible times given names had greater significance. One's name was almost equivalent to one's self. The name of God was not to be spoken casually. There was "magic" in names.)

In contrast with signs, theological symbols bear a necessary relation to the thing symbolized. Nothing else will quite do. The symbol is essentially irreplaceable. Professor Tillich speaks of the symbol as "participating" in the thing symbolized. There are qualities in the symbol that necessarily correspond to that to which the symbol points.

The father "symbol" for God is a case in point—not just the word. It could as well be *padre, vater, wader, pater,* or whatever. (Abba, or daddy, is a bit familiar for the Almighty.) These could all be "signs." But the father role is a true symbol. The father-child relationship has qualities that are also those of the God-man relation. Sigmund Freud branded religion an illusion (*The Future of an Illusion*) based on half-forgotten images of our fathers that we project into the heavens. He was correct in his observation, but mistaken in his interpretation. God created fathers to provide an experience matrix that could be the basis for a child's later perception of his or her heavenly Father. Ellen White tells us that parents are God to their children during their early years. This is so because the parental role is a true symbol, "participating" in the reality to which it points.

Time is an important symbol. Time is uncontrollable, incomprehensible, indefinable, and shares in these qualities with God. Augustine said of time, "When I think about it I don't know what it is. When I don't think about it I know what it is." As one points to one moment it is already another, like Heraclitus' stream. Time is the stuff of life. Time takes priority over all else. Time is sovereign. As to God so every creature is subject to time.

This is the essence of that special time that God created on the seventh day. Six days He created things in space. On the seventh day

He created a moment of time and called it the Sabbath, a time for resting in His sovereign love.

The ineffable qualities of Sabbath time serve to condition God's rational creatures in their relation to their Creator. Note this in connection with the difficulty experienced in establishing the temporal boundaries of the Sabbath day. The seven-day week differs essentially from all the other natural time-markers. A year, a month, even a day are all based on natural phenomena. But the Sabbath day depends upon a weekly cycle, and there is nothing in nature that establishes such a cycle. A Sabbath day might be derived from human need for recurring physical and spiritual respite. This has sometimes been put forward by Sunday observers as the basis for Sunday observance (e.g., in Marva J. Dawn, *Keeping the Sabbath Wholly*). But *the* seventh-day Sabbath of the Bible exists only by an act of the divine will—because God said so. And He can say so because He is Creator.

It is difficult to find *any* day everywhere on a round, revolving, irregularly surfaced world. Genesis tells us that a day is an evening followed by a morning, and Leviticus tells us that "from even unto even, shall ye celebrate your sabbath" (Lev. 23:32, KJV). Which day in the succession was the Sabbath day was revealed in the falling of the manna at Sinai, the customary behavior of Jesus, and in the history of a people. (If one wishes to know which day is the Sabbath, all one has to do is ask the nearest Jew. He or she can at least direct you to a rabbi.) That all sounds simple and straightforward, and it is for most of the world, most of the time, but . . . There is a lesson here.

When I was a boy I lived with my Adventist family in Provo, Utah. Provo was a small town in those days. It nestled in a valley at the edge of a large freshwater lake, largely surrounded by the Wasatch Mountains. To the east of town was a two-tiered series of peaks, the higher ones behind with a somewhat lower range in front. Across Utah Lake to the west of town there was an even lower range with rounded tops that were often silhouetted in the setting sun.

One of the "games" we played in those days (game is hardly an appropriate name for such serious business) involved deciding when the Sabbath began and ended. When did the sun set? When the sun visibly dropped behind the mountains to the west? Or when its rays no longer lingered on the mountains to the east? And if the latter, and one were near the mountains, when the sun's rays disappeared from the lower prominences in front or from the peaks behind that might not even be visible? The exercise was academic, of course, on a cloudy day.

How one answered these questions depended somewhat on what one had in mind. If one wanted more playtime on Friday evening, the higher peaks were the way to go. If one wanted the Sabbath to end earlier on Saturday evening so as to get on with other things, one preferred the hills across the lake.

Eventually the problem was solved by the publishing of sunset tables in the *Pacific Union Recorder*. After that, even weather was no hindrance to proper Sabbath observance.

It was somewhat disquieting to be told some years later that those sunset tables were derived from a governmental agency's calculation of sunset at sea level! Provo's elevation was more than 4,000 feet, which meant that we continued to be bathed in lingering sunlight for some time after sunset at sea level. Could it be that for all those years we were not keeping an accurate Sabbath?

It was also somewhat disquieting to learn later that even had we been standing on an ocean beach watching the sun dip below the watery horizon, we would still not be keeping an accurate Sabbath because of atmospheric refraction of the sun's rays. Because of the bending of the sun's rays by the atmosphere, the sun was actually below the horizon before it disappeared from view. (I have no idea whether smog would compound the difficulty.) It is difficult to capture sunset time on an irregularly surfaced earth, to say, "There it is. Now we have it." Time is like that.

And it becomes worse. I grew up and went to college, where I finished the ministerial course and eventually became a pastor in Fairbanks, Alaska. Fairbanks is about 100 miles south of the Arctic Circle, that imaginary line north of which there are neither sunrises nor sunsets for a considerable part of each year, depending on how far north one goes. How do Sabbathkeepers find their Sabbath where there are no sunsets?

Many years later I was invited to give a series of lectures in Sydney, Australia. I boarded a Qantas airliner at San Francisco on a Thursday evening, expecting to arrive at Sydney airport sometime on Friday forenoon. I was scheduled to deliver the sermon at Sydney Adventist Hospital on Sabbath morning. I slept most of the time while flying.

When I disembarked at Sydney, I was surprised to find a delegation waiting to hurry me through customs so that I could arrive at the church in time to deliver the sermon! (Very confusing. I was suffering from a huge dose of jet lag. The sun was in the wrong side of the heavens, funny-looking birds were singing strange songs, everybody spoke with an accent—and it was the wrong day of the week! Luckily, my sermon was written out, or I would never have been able to get through it.) But what had happened to Friday? How did I move directly from Thursday into Saturday without knowing it?

Somewhere between Honolulu and Sydney I had lost Friday. Ah, of course, the date line. I had slept through the date line. How can one keep track of the Sabbath when, traveling one way around the world, one can move from Friday directly into Sunday and when traveling the other way, one can have two Sabbaths back to back?

There is more. Precision in Sabbathkeeping presupposes an unaltered rhythm of weekly cycles clear back to Creation week. How can we be certain that the cycles were not broken or lost somewhere back in prehistory before people were keeping track of such things? And of course, we cannot be sure, except with the kind of faith that asserts that God would surely know what He was doing when He reestablished the Sabbath at Sinai. The manna was clearly time-specific. Surely an entire people would not lose track of a weekly cycle after Sinai. And surely our Lord was not confused over which day was the Sabbath after all His efforts to purify it.

Unfortunately, there are at least two places on the globe where in modern times the weekly cycle was compromised. December 31, 1844, a Tuesday, I think, was dropped from the weekly calendar (not just as a date but as a day of the week) in the Spanish-dominated Philippine Islands by ecclesiastical decree in order to bring the holy days of the Philippines into harmony with other nearby island groups dominated by the Portuguese. The Portuguese had explored the world from east to west, and then later the Spanish had explored from west to east, and the two came to overlap in the region of the Philippines. Because they had circumnavigated the rotating world in opposite directions, their calendars were out of synchrony by one day. Fortunately, the dropping of the day put the Philippines on the correct side of the date line, which was formally established some 40 years later.

The same thing happened in Alaska. The Russians came from the west and the other Europeans from the east, and again they were one day out of synchrony. When Alaska was sold to America, the ruling Russian Orthodox patriarch told the members of his church, of whom there were a fair number in Alaska, to adjust the days of the week so as to have the same Sundays and holy days as the Americans. How is a Sabbathkeeper to discover a day that can so easily be shifted about by prelates and accommodated to humanly established date lines?

What day is the Sabbath in the Philippines and Alaska? And in Tonga, where the issue was never resolved? On Tonga, Sabbathkeepers and Sundaykeepers go to church on the same day, only the Sabbathkeepers call it Saturday and the Sundaykeepers call it Sunday. On Kwajalein atoll, downrange from Vandenberg missile base, if one is employed by the U.S. government, he or she will have one Sabbath.

But if he or she is a national or other inhabitant of the atoll, he or she will likely have another. The government has chosen to place the atoll on the American side of the date line (for missile-testing reasons, I presume). The atoll is actually on the other.

How did the date line come to be precisely where it is? It had to be somewhere on a revolving round world. At least there is a lot of open water and very few land masses where it is. For centuries that region was roughly designated in practice, but not until 1884 at a formal international maritime conference was it located at the 180th meridian, where it is today. Appropriate doglegs were also devised at the conference so that it would avoid major land masses such as Alaska and New Zealand.

And why the 180th meridian? Besides the expanse of water, it was on the opposite side of the world from the Royal Observatory at Greenwich, England. Given the maritime supremacy of the United Kingdom at the time, it seemed the logical thing to do. Established custom had also made almost everyone concerned with shipping comfortable with the location. But, the question is Can Sabbathkeepers feel comfortable with establishing the Sabbath on so mundane an authority as an international maritime organization?

There are more problems (the thought of keeping the Sabbath on an orbiting space station fairly boggles the mind), but that is probably sufficient to make the point. How can God expect us—at least, all of us—to take seriously the "keeping" of something so difficult to establish as the Sabbath on a round world? And if some of us cannot, should it be expected of any of us? I have also pursued the issue at considerable length to press home the point that time, especially Sabbath time, is not fully under human control. It is thus a true symbol of God, who is likewise not under our control.

To illustrate this, let us propose another kind of symbol for Creation, one more nearly a "sign." Let us suppose that God spoke to Adam and Eve that evening of the sixth day, drawing their attention to a large black rock in the midst of the garden. "See, now, this great black stone? I have blessed and hallowed it to be a perpetual reminder that I have created it and all rocks, trees, the sky, the waters, and animals of all kinds, and finally created you. You and your children must keep this rock holy."

It is not difficult to imagine the scenario that would follow this announcement. For a time they would be aware that the rock was a memorial of God's creative activity. Little by little, however, their worship would be transferred from God to the rock. It would be endowed with magical powers, dressed in costly brocades with gold, silver, and jeweled ornaments, and worshiped with elaborate rituals and circumambulations. Eventually priestly entrepreneurs would chip pieces off the rock to sell to the faithful to be placed on the dashboards of their automobiles to protect them on the freeways, or placed in their breast pockets to deflect bullets in battle.

Possessing a "piece of the rock" would offer great advantages. For one, it could be carried wherever one wished and used in whatever manner one desired. Human beings would have complete control of the rock. This is the precise reason that God, when He wished to reinforce the sense of His creative sovereignty, chose a true "symbol"—the Sabbath—rather than a mere "sign." The essence of idolatry is human control of the gods, using them to serve our own ends. In true worship the creature serves the Creator's ends.

The Sabbath symbol was chosen because *Homo sapiens* is also *Homo symbolicus*. We are symbol-using creatures by nature. The use of symbols forms the basis for our reasoning and communication. Practically all reasoning after the development of our language structure is verbal reasoning. Words are our most common symbols (or signs). Symbols are also important creators and reinforcers of attitudes. Religious people have always known this. An attitude of worship can be created by a variety of symbolic objects and activities.

That is the purpose and function of the Sabbath symbol. It is not an end in itself. Adventists do not worship the Sabbath. They worship the Creator of the Sabbath, as well as the Creator of everything else. The essence of Sabbathkeeping is not an attitude toward a day but an attitude toward the God of the day. The essence of the final conflict between those who receive the mark of the beast and those bearing the seal of God is not so much between one day and another—for instance, Saturday versus Sunday—as it is a conflict between those who place God first in their lives (the essence of worship) and those who choose self-sufficiency apart from God. The Sabbath was created to provide a powerful motivation for true worship.

Note how this truth comes through in relation to the difficulty we have experienced in identifying the Sabbath-symbol on a rotating round world. It is really a nonproblem. Obedience can only be as specific as the command. God said not one word about Arctic or Antarctic circles or the date line. If He had, we would be privileged to exercise the same care about these as we are expected to show toward seven-day weeks and sunsets as an expression of worship. He was clear enough about Sabbath beginnings and endings. What of these other things? Putting God first, conforming to His expressed will, is a way of life that touches all dimensions of life, and it is expressed as obeying where and when God has clearly spoken, and doing the best we can to approximate His will where He has not. This is the proper posture of the creatures toward their Creator.

True Sabbathkeeping touches the whole of life. The Sabbath sanctifies the week. One cannot be dishonest on Monday and truly keep the Sabbath, because Sabbathkeeping is essentially a posture toward God that is not a one-day-in-seven kind of activity.

Could one lose one's Sabbath by becoming confused about the day of the week? Suppose that you are shipwrecked and washed up on a beach on an uninhabited island. You are alive but are unconscious for an unknown period of time. You have no idea what day of the week it is. Would you lose your Sabbath? No. Not in essence. The principle of doing the best one can would take over, and you would simply start counting. Today is day one, the next day is day two, and so on until day seven, which you would keep as the Sabbath. God would honor your Sabbathkeeping because it would be done out of faithfulness to Him and the best you could do. But in this faithfulness, the first question you would ask the boatload of sailors sent to rescue you would be "What day is it?"

Suppose they would say "It's Thursday," and you were counting "day three" on your homemade calendar. Quickly, according to the above principle, you would make the adjustment.

For nearly the first decade of its existence, the Adventist Church kept the Sabbath from 6:00 p.m. to 6:00 a.m., probably on the counsel of Joseph Bates, a retired sea captain who knew something of date lines and such. After further study, they found the "from even until even" text and changed over in order to be as close to God's revealed will as possible.

North of the Arctic Circle we kept the Sabbath from noon until noon in winter and from midnight until midnight in summer. Those times were convenient, since that was near the last time we saw the sun set and would be near the next time we saw it when sunsets started coming around again. Again, our posture toward God led us to come as close to His revealed will as possible—as a matter of principle. The Sabbath was not given for the worshiping of a day. It was established for the worshiping of God, our sovereign Creator and Redeemer, for putting Him first in our lives.

The difficulty in finding the Sabbath on a rotating round world is but another reminder of our creatureliness and finitude. Time, especially sacred time, is not under our control. Neither is God. It is in His plan that we should experience a sense of uneasiness, even helplessness, as we try to take independent charge of things. "It is not for you to know the times or the seasons, which the Father hath put in his own power" (Acts 1:7, KJV).

The message of the three angels is clearly that God is sovereign in time and eternity. Graciously He has given us a symbol in time to remind us of that essential truth.

One final word about symbols. As has been suggested, a symbol, to function as a symbol, must "point" or refer to something beyond itself. In the present case, the Sabbath "points" to the Creator. But it must also *be seen* to point. That is, if no one knows that it is pointing or to what it is pointing, it is meaningless as a symbol. This is the reason that the keeping of the Sabbath involves refraining from certain activities and becoming active in others. The not-working was not so much because of a need to rest, at least for God (and certainly not for Adam and Eve, who had come on the scene only the day before), as it was to make the day different, to set it apart, to call attention to it so that it could serve its intended function. In other words, the symbol must have *being* before it can have *function*.

This fact could give us some guidance regarding appropriate behavior on the Sabbath. Almost any action or activity that serves to increase reverence, veneration, respect, admiration, and devotion to God (recall Webster's definition of worship) is appropriate Sabbath behavior. In addition, any of these that help make the day "different" may also be appropriate. To illustrate: An emergency room physician whose everyday activities are the kind of activities that would also be appropriate on the Sabbath could lose his Sabbath. However, if he were perceptive to what we are talking about and wished to protect his Sabbath, he might just do the right things differently—different garb, perhaps different music in the background, different conversation, more time spent with other aspects of patient care, different meals, etc.

Judaism at its best could teach Seventh-day Adventists a great deal about calling attention to the Sabbath. It will help some if we can remember that keeping the Sabbath is, for a prophetic movement, primarily a call to worship. We should be as creative as we can about the details and share them with each other.

CHAPTER SEVEN

That They May Be One

A S WE have seen, the first angel's call to worship the Creator and Sustainer of all that is has many and varied implications. Ellen White referred to one of these in her rejection (cited in the previous chapter—see *Testimonies*, vol. 8, pp. 259, 260) of the traditional antinomy of natural and supernatural as "false science."

Some of our ancestors thought in terms of a two-story universe (three-story if one included the underworld). In such a universe God's activities were largely confined to the upper floor. But an essential theme of the prophetic movement's message is that God is at work at all levels of reality. Universal and one are consonant. The distinction should be between God's "usual" and His "unusual" (miraculous) works rather than between natural and supernatural. It is one of the privileges of this movement to be able to point to God's presence in the ordinary and everyday as well as in the extraordinary. See how this comes through in another key passage that is in complete harmony with the earlier one.

> God desires that His workers in every line shall look to Him as the Giver of all they possess. [Recall what the term "worker" indicates in traditional Adventist speech and practice, that is, denominational employee. Note its wider meaning here.] All right inventions and improvements have their source in Him who is wonderful in

counsel and excellent in working. The skillful touch of the physician's hand, his power over nerve and muscle, his knowledge of the delicate organism of the body, is the wisdom of divine power, to be used in behalf of the suffering. The skill with which the carpenter uses the hammer, the strength with which the blacksmith makes the anvil ring, comes from God. He has entrusted men with talents, and He expects them to look to Him for counsel. Whatever we do, in whatever department of the work we are placed, He desires to control our minds that we may do perfect work.

Religion and business are not two separate things; they are one. Bible religion is to be interwoven with all we do or say. Divine and human agencies are to combine in temporal as well as in spiritual achievements. They are to be united in all human pursuits, in mechanical and agricultural labors, in mercantile and scientific enterprises (*Christ's Object Lessons*, pp. 349, 350).

Thomas Chalmers once said, "If it be the characteristic of a worldly man that he desecrates what is holy, it should be of the Christian to consecrate what is secular, and to recognize a present and presiding divinity in all things" (in Mead's *Encyclopedia of Religious Quotations*, p. 226).

Acknowledging that God is Creator and Sustainer of all things means that whenever we act in a manner so as to assist, support, and cooperate with the processes of "creation," we do "God-work." Ambroise Paré, the renowned French barber-surgeon, was correct when he said some 400 years ago, "I dress the wounds, God heals them." So is the scientist who "thinks God's thoughts after Him."

But creation includes more than starry heavens, physiological processes, birds, and flowers. God also created human interactions. To cooperate with and support nature at the level of family and community is also to assist God at work. Parents properly rearing their children are doing the work of God, and so are the people who strive to make their communities better places in which to live. No such activity is intrinsically "secular." There are no intrinsically sacred or profane professions or vocations, providing they are related to the divine creation. There are only sacred or profane people in them. The laboratory can be as holy as the chancel, the marketplace as sacred as the sanctuary, and there is holiness in housework, being a parent, or constructing a fine piece of furniture or a home if God is creatively present.

True, we set apart some callings such as the gospel ministry by special ordination to remind us of the sacredness of all legitimate callings, just as God set apart the Sabbath day to remind us of the sacredness of all time. We may also think of a "sanctified" prophetic movement in these terms, a movement called, set apart, to serve "God's people" all around the world. Each of these functions as a true symbol.

Such thinking could change the way we look at "lay" and professional workers. Elimination of the distinction between the natural and supernatural in the matter of church polity could serve to diminish the artificial gulf between such workers. Wholeness could render the distinction one of function rather than of value. Administrative roles in the church, for example, could be based on calling and competence rather than on artificial sacerdotal authority. There is no essential reason that high church office should be not filled by trained administrators regardless of whether or not they have come up through the ranks of the ordained ministry.

What a difference it would make if all God's children always carried out their, even quite ordinary, activities with a sense of the divine presence! One can hardly imagine a more radical circumstance, one more calculated utterly to transform life on this planet. But that's just what radical monotheism, the belief that God is Creator and Sustainer of everything, is all about. (The tragedy is that a people with such a message seem often to have understood this truth no better than most other men and women in the world.)

Another response to the monotheistic premise has found a much wider acceptance in Adventism. From almost the beginning, concern for physical well-being was central to Adventist belief and practice. Partly this was because of our Protestant heritage. (One of Wesley's most widely distributed books had to do with healthful living—much of it nonsense, unfortunately.) The thrift, hard work, and Spartan lifestyle of the so-called Protestant ethic rendered self-indulgence and indolence sins to be shunned.

But mainly our conditionalist doctrine of humankind, what we used to call "the state of the dead" doctrine, shaped our concern for the physical body. According to this view, human beings have no personal existence apart from the physical body. Death is an unconscious sleep. There is nothing in humans, no immortal soul, that guarantees the future. In the face of death, all people confront the ultimate manifestation of their creaturely dependence. The only hope for life after death is the restored, translated or resurrected body, transformed by God at the second coming of Jesus. As the gospel song says, because Jesus lives we can face tomorrow.

The term that describes this kind of understanding is "wholism." (Please note the spelling. There is a loose, countering collection of New Age—far-out, anti-scientific nonsense—floating around that is spelled "holism," which, based on a different set of presuppositions, only faintly resembles the wholism of the Adventist message.) To use one of Paul Tillich's weighty phrases, a human being is a "multidimensional unity."

> In every dimension of life, all dimensions are potentially or actually present; he does not consist of levels of being, but he is a unity that unites all dimensions. This doctrine stands against the dualistic theory, which sees

man as composed of soul and body; of body and mind; or body, soul, and spirit, etc. Man is one, uniting within himself all dimensions of life. . . . The multidimensional unity of life in man calls for a multidimensional concept of health, of disease, and healing, but in such a way that it becomes obvious that in each dimension all the others are present (Paul Tillich, "The Meaning of Health," *Perspectives in Biology and Medicine*, Autumn 1961).

The point of the wholistic understanding of humanness is that whatever happens to any individual person in any particular happens in some way to the whole. Mind affects body, body affects mind, and factors in the environment affect both mind and body.

(The dualistic theory, which professor Tillich rejects [as do Adventists], has of late ostensibly found support in "out of the body" experiences reported by individuals who have been resuscitated from near death. [See Raymond A. Moody, Jr., *Life After Life* (1976). See also the author's *Is Death for Real?* (1981).] Individuals experiencing this phenomenon report that they had left their bodies and looked back at them [psychiatrists call this autoscopy] while the rescue team was trying to resuscitate them. They insist that they saw lights and other things, suggesting some kind of transport to a spirit world where the bodies they left behind were superfluous. The fact that the phenomenon is also experienced in connection with drugs [such as LSD], anesthetics, carbon dioxide inhalation, acute emotional stress states, and even in otherwise perfectly normal people, suggests other explanations, including the accumulation of central nervous system metabolites in an individual whose circulation has been compromised in cardiac arrest. The resulting experience may be a psychochemically induced illusion or hallucination. If this is true, it could support an exactly opposite conclusion. It may simply demonstrate the validity of the wholistic understanding. The body may actually be influencing the psyche rather than being dissociated from it.)

The wholistic view, which is so central to the prophetic movement's message, has conditioned mental and physical health-consciousness in a number of important ways. Very early it affected the church institutionally. Given the size of the church at the time, an incredible number of sanitariums, hospitals, treatment rooms, etc., were established in America and around the world, including two medical schools (serially) and many schools of nursing. Battle Creek Sanitarium virtually became "the tail that wagged the dog" for a time. These health-related institutions became the best-known feature of Adventism around the world.

Unfortunately, over the course of their history some of these institutions became associated with other ideals than wholeness, making it difficult to think of their thrust as an expression of a radically monotheistic conception of God. Some of them are now indistinguishable from institutions operating on quite different—including entrepreneurial—premises, and we are, as of this writing, in big financial trouble in some quarters. Adventists may want to reexamine whether it is appropriate to continue operating institutions that drift too far from the ground on which they were established.

The concept of wholeness has also made an impact on personal health goals. People jog in the rain at 6:00 in the morning and eat low-fat, low-cholesterol, low-sodium diets for a variety of reasons. Running and low-fat diets make for slim waistlines, slender thighs, and nice legs. Such a program makes one look good. It also make one feel good, as every jogger knows (those endorphins). For those who are good at it, at least, it can be a source of competitive self-esteem. It makes for robust cardiovascular health. Joggers live longer. (Nonjoggers say it only seems like it!) All these are good reasons, but apparently not enough, to get all the potatoes off the couch.

The message of the three angels posits concern for physical health squarely within the general theme of worship of the Creator. If one worships God, one must respect His creation, of which the body is the very epitome. It is an affront to the Creator to abuse His creation. No higher motivation to healthful living can be envisioned. The call to worship the Creator and Sustainer is a call to vibrant health. (At least as vibrant as is possible at this stage of the planet's history. It is not a sin to be sick, but it is only a sin to be sicker than one needs to be.)

The laws of health are also God's laws. They are revealed to us as aids to self-fulfilling physical and mental well-being. That some may wrest these laws by making them legalistic evidences of personal piety, and thus serving as coping behavior for unresolved or even unrecognized guilt, should not be allowed to obscure that important truth. (There is a certain dissonance in "practicing health reform if it kills me.")

One of the reassuring developments of modern medicine is the degree to which it has come to confirm the Adventist diet and lifestyle. As a consequence, never has it been so easy to find a vegetarian meal in a public restaurant or to enjoy a smokeless flight on United Airlines. Many other voices are speaking our lines now in matters of health, and sometimes better than we.

But there is a difference. There is the matter of motivation. The reasons that one does something largely condition one's success or failure. To look after physical, mental, and social health as an expression of worship is far more likely to ensure the faithfulness, perseverance, and upbeat attitude that good health requires. (I have no idea if any, or how many, Adventists include the worship of God in their pursuit of health. The point is, they ought to. It is an essential part of their prophetic message.)

There is another sound marching mightily in the tops of the balsam trees (1 Chron. 14:15) these days. In contrast with their longstanding interest in health, Adventists strangely have only lately become interested in environmental matters. Their call to worship the Creator and Sustainer of everything that is should have placed them in the forefront of this issue from the very beginning.

Their failure to be involved is probably related to their having only recently come on the scene. Movements of recent origin, often called "sects," tend to be anti-establishment. They are often protest movements, protesting against what they see to be powerful, authoritarian, evil forces. Their ethic is more likely to be personal than social. They tend to stress individual rights and responsibilities. They are likely to be death on personal vices, such as smoking, card-playing, dancing, the theater, and sex, while ignoring the vices of social injustice, human rights, poverty, and educational deprivation. This is partly so because social problems call for societal rather than personal solutions. Typically the sect has little time for or interest in, political action.

But most of the world's environmental problems are too complex for individuals or small groups to handle. Cleaning up our rivers, lakes, and sky involves the expenditure of enormous amounts of effort and money, and there are no quick fixes. It will call for massive and persistent governmental effort applied over the long haul.

Meanwhile, there is a role for prophetic minorities to play. Mainly, "prophets" are called to do what prophets have always done, to call attention to the disasters that threaten and to stimulate corrective action on the part of the larger society. Unfortunately, most *secular* "prophets" have their own agendas. Too often they espouse "in" causes as a way of filling otherwise vacuous lives. (The students of a Southern university organized a "float-in" protest against the pollution of a local river. They floated down the river in rafts, on inner tubes, in kayaks, canoes, etc., drinking beer, singing, shouting, and carrying placards. After the "float-in," the authorities picked up 100 tons of junk and garbage from the banks of the river—piles of beer and soft-drink cans, plastic containers, inner tubes, and clothing, including one bra.

These college young people were not serious about the environment. They were interested only in "having a ball" or, some of them, in having a "cause." They were like the Klondike gold miner who, having made a strike, proceeded to put it back in the ground as it were and began looking for more. When asked about this he replied, "It wasn't the gold I wanted. It was the finding of it."

Again, the question is one of motivation. Adventists did not define this issue as they did the matter of health. They should have. It was looking them directly in the face as a necessary corollary and consequence of worshiping the Creator. This is the message of our first parents' having been given dominion over the whole earth "to work it and take care of it" (Gen. 2:15). It is also the message of Revelation 11:18, warning about the destruction of "those who destroy the earth." To repeat, it is an affront to God to abuse His creation.

The environmentalist tragedy is that we know what to do to clean things up, to restore them, and to prevent further despoiling. What is presently missing—at all levels, from individuals up to the highest authorities in the land—is the will to do what we know we ought to do. To worship the Creator is to bring to conscious awareness the fact that it is *God's* sky, *His* streams and lakes, *His* rivers and oceans, *His* forests, *His* soil and wetlands, *His* earth.

This consciousness could make an enormous difference to those who have a heart to listen. But whether or not anyone listens, a prophet must sound his or her alarums. A prophetic movement must speak out. Concern for the world around us is also a part of the essential message of the three angels.

CHAPTER EIGHT

A New Creature

THERE is another manifestation of Creator-worship that especially demonstrates the principle of synthesis in the message of the three angels. (Recall that it is a synthesis of ideas—the way it all comes together, rather than innovation—that characterizes the essence of the prophetic movement's message.) This has to do with the fact that salvation involves creation. The psalmist cried out in the anguish of his guilt, "Create in me a pure heart, O God" (Ps. 51:10), and Paul writes in his second letter to the Corinthians, "If anyone is in Christ, he is a new creation" (2 Cor. 5:17).

The question of how people are saved has been a theological battleground for ages past, and it is currently at issue in the Seventh-day Adventist Church. The matter is raised here not only because it is important, but also because it is an area in which the essence of the Adventist synthesis (the underlying theme of our whole discussion) has something special to say.

I do not expect to exhaust the subject in so brief a space, nor do I expect that what I have to say will be welcomed in all quarters. On this topic it may be appropriate to keep our theology "on the wing" as it used to be said of Karl Barth's almost endless flow of theological nuances.

Ellen White says, "It will take the whole of eternity for man to understand the plan of redemption" (*The Seventh-day Adventist Bible Commentary*, Ellen G. White Comments, vol. 6, p. 1115). Certainty can wait. Eternity is a long time. Meanwhile, to one of Luther's purported statements, *"Hier stehe ich! Ich kann nicht anders* [Here I stand. I cannot do otherwise]," I would only add, ". . . at the moment." What follows is for me "present truth," to be shared as one shares a journey.

Four elements make up the salvation message committed to this people in Revelation 14. We have spoken of one of them at some length, the call to worship the Creator. This call alone and by itself is a vital factor in the understandings that are so essential to this prophetic movement's identity, but it gains its most fundamental thrust in combination with three other elements. The gospel (verse 6), the time of judgment (verse 7), and obedience (verse 12).

By the gospel is meant simply the "good news" about God, what Ellen White apparently had in mind when she wrote, "The Lord has proclaimed Himself to be 'merciful and gracious, long-suffering, and abundant in goodness and truth.' . . . The message of justification by faith is the third angel's message. . . . 'It is the third angel's message in verity' " (*Selected Messages*, book 1, p. 372). This is what is to be proclaimed "to every nation, tribe, language and people" (Rev. 14:6). In Ellen White's words: "At this time a message from God is to be proclaimed, a message illuminating in its influence and saving in its power. His character is to be made known. Into the darkness of the world is to be shed the light of His glory, the light of His goodness, mercy, and truth" (*Christ's Object Lessons*, p. 415).

But the "good news" is also about *us* — if what we have said about the message as "synthesis" is correct. It concerns, and is not to be separated from, our patient obedience to God's commandments. Revelation 14:12 speaks of "saints [people who are set apart] who obey God's commandments," which may not seem like such good news to most of us when we look at our face in the mirror. Perfect obedience has always seemed an impossible dream. Many troubled Christians have wrestled with the high moral standard suggested by such statements as "Be perfect, therefore, as your heavenly Father is perfect" (Matt. 5:48) or even in the three angels' text, "They are blameless" (Rev. 14:5; KJV—"In their mouth was found no guile"). It is said of Jesus our example that He "knew no sin" (2 Cor. 5:21, KJV).

Adventist believers have borne the additional burden of statements such as the following from the pen of their prophet, Ellen G. White:

> The condition of eternal life is now just what it has always been—just what it was in Paradise before the fall of our first parents—perfect obedience to the law of God, perfect righteousness (*Steps to Christ*, p. 62).

> Christ is waiting with longing desire for the manifestation of Himself in His church. When the character of Christ shall be perfectly reproduced in His people, then He will come to claim them as His own (*Christ's Object Lessons*, p. 69).

We all know how hard it is to achieve perfect obedience, what a struggle is involved every day, and how few of us are making any kind of go of it. Most of us feel the full weight of Jesus' words in response to the query "Lord, are only a few people going to be saved?" He replied, "Make every effort to enter through the narrow door, because many, I tell you, will try to enter and will not be able to" (Luke 13:23, 24). Much of the time the apostle Paul states the case for us in his confession, "I know that nothing good lives in me, that is, in my sinful nature. For I have the desire to do what is good, but I cannot carry it out. For what I do is not the good I want to do; no, the evil I do not want to do—this I keep on doing" (Rom. 7:18, 19). It is not difficult to identify with the character in Karl Menninger's story.

> On a sunny day in September 1972, a stern-faced, plainly dressed man could be seen standing still on a street corner in the busy Chicago Loop. As pedestrians hurried by on their way to lunch or business, he would solemnly lift his right arm, and pointing to the person

nearest him, intone the single word "GUILTY!"

Then, without any change of expression, he would resume his stiff stance for a few moments before repeating the gesture. Then, again, the inexorable raising of his arm, the pointing, and the solemn pronouncing of the one word "GUILTY!"

The effect of this strange *j'accuse* pantomime on the passing strangers was extraordinary, almost eerie. They would stare at him, hesitate, look away, look at each other, and then at him again, then hurriedly continue on their ways.

One man, turning to another who was my informant, exclaimed: "But how did *he* know?" (*Whatever Became of Sin?* pp. 1, 2).

And if the Second Coming depends upon a perfect reproduction of Christ in His people, surely we are in for trouble as far as a finished work is concerned! How many people do you know whose characters meet Christ's exalted standard? I know a great many relatively "good" people—individuals, in fact, with whom I would be happy to spend eternity, but not a single one I would confuse with Jesus.

Surely the foregoing statement from *Christ's Object Lessons* does not mean what it seems to say. (There is another way of thinking of that passage, by the way. Back in the days when Chairman Mao was running things in mainland China thousands of Communist youth were gathered at a meeting in Beijing. They filled the seats of a vast stadium, one side of which was set apart for a special production. On that side all the attendees held in their hands cards, each of a single color. On signal they all held up their cards, and there appeared a huge portrait of their leader. It took all of them together to make the portrait. Could that be what a perfect reproduction of Christ in His people actually means?)

It is against this reality that many Adventists feel apprehensive over a new emphasis on substituting His righteousness for our unrighteousness, or to put it another way, quoting from a popular bumper sticker, "Christians are not perfect, they are just forgiven." (I suspect that M. L. Andreasen was one of the first among us to call this "new theology," although "new" it surely isn't.)

The new emphasis seems to suggest to some that our perennial struggle with sin is irrelevant. It is difficult enough to be good without introducing a "cheap grace" that makes human effort at being good seem not only irrelevant but frivolous. Surely, they say, what we need is not a way to feel more comfortable in our sins but help in gaining the victory over them.

The "grace" thus proffered could even seem to be a little dangerous. Will we really feel comfortable with having people with us in heaven who have made it by celestial magic rather than by becoming the kind of people it was safe to save? That thief on the cross (praise God that he will be there)—surely we will want him to have quit being a thief! The absolute trust that characterizes the atmosphere of Paradise would render it highly vulnerable to unregenerate thieves—or unregenerate anyone else. (But since we will have all our wants supplied in heaven, perhaps there will be no temptation to steal. Or is stealing more than just a question of satisfying wants or needs?)

One of the things that we can say about heaven, almost by definition, is that it is a place of abundant goodness—in everyone, us included. But just *how good* do we have to be to get there? How much character refinement is necessary to render us "safe to save"? This is a question all of us have probably asked in one way or another at some time. If I were to die at this moment, would I be good enough to be taken to heaven? It is a sobering question, one something like the words of a lovely Christian song we used to sing in the youth tent in the old days, "Are You Ready for Jesus to Come?"

Well, how good do we have to be to be ready? That's a good question. Unfortunately, there is no easy answer to it. Human goodness is a highly relative quality or set of qualities. There are so many factors involved in making us the kind of people we are. For instance, the kind of parents we've had. We could all do better if we were permitted to choose our parents. And it is not only a question of nature. Nurture also plays a role, as do the surroundings, the physical and social environment, the family. I have friends who, because of being born into a good family, began life already halfway up the ladder. I have other friends who have had to struggle all the way from the bottom. Lincoln, perhaps, had something like this in mind when he observed that the importance of a man was not to be judged by how high he climbed but by how far.

I remember two brothers. Born of the same parents, sharing the same home environment, one of them seemed destined for conflict and struggle from earliest childhood. He was given to terrifying mood shifts, violent anger, and profound depression. During adolescence his sexual drives fairly drove him up the walls. He was always in trouble. The other brother, by contrast, always seemed to sail on smooth waters. He was sweet and lovable, even-tempered, self-controlled, never hostile. Perhaps he had more difficulties than were obvious, but if so they were well concealed. Which one was "good enough" for heaven? (One is tempted to favor the troubled lad, who surely had little enough of heaven here on earth.) Is heaven in our genes, our chromosomes, our hormones, our heredity?

Then there's intelligence. The intelligent often experience moral and intellectual struggles of which simple folks have little comprehension. Is it not an advantage to be born with meager gifts?

And time. Perhaps it would be well for all of us to die in the innocence of childhood (assuming that there is such a thing). On the other hand, living to a ripe old age could allow more time for character building. Some temptations seem to lose their thrust with age. (Is there such a thing as being sanctified by senility?) Unfortunately, the reverse is also true. Sometimes age brings out the worst in people. An old adage says that with aging we become "more so," that is, qualities we possessed earlier in life tend to become more pronounced with advancing years. Old age may be youth in caricature.

Aging can make a travesty of youth. A sweet little grandmother I know began to swear "like a muleskinner" as she aged. A patient who was formerly a highly respected and honored Presbyterian minister developed senile dementia late in life. On each visit his sweet minister's wife was shocked and humiliated by his foul language and coarse attempts at humor. She would blush and cry, "Doctor, why does he do this?" Repeatedly I had to reassure her that I understood and that he was not responsible for his personality changes.

Ah, and what about the right time? Surely one must avoid having one's fatal heart attack during an angry encounter with a neighbor or while having a sexual affair with one's best friend's wife or when breaking the Sabbath!

A psychiatrist colleague once told me of a patient suffering from a cyclothymic personality. He would have prolonged mood swings lasting months at a time. When he was on the down side of things, his behavior became inconsistent with church membership, and they would have to let him go. But when he was back on the crest, things would pick up, and he would be welcomed back into the church family. Three times he had been disfellowshipped and three times restored. One could only hope that his final moment would come when he was on the top of a wave.

When I was a boy one of the arguments against theater attendance was that the place might catch fire—or the roof fall in—and "How would you like to be in such a place then?"

By now we should begin to suspect that there is something amiss in all this. How can salvation be at the mercy of something so trivial as an accident of birth, time and place, age, hormones, mood swings, native mental acuity, and the like? Goodness is a relative thing, almost as varied as the number of persons seeking it, but is there no standard against which individuals can be judged worthy or unworthy of salvation?

No, because salvation is a gift, and a gift is not something one either deserves or fails to deserve.

How, then, is personal goodness related to salvation? It has been a part of the synthesis of Adventism to see grace and works as integral parts of one complete whole, avoiding cheap grace on the one hand and salvation by works on the other. Paul and James both belong in the Book.

Actually, the question "How good do we *have* to be?" is not the proper question. We should be asking instead, "How good do we *get* to be?" "Have to be" implies the imposition of an unwanted burden, whereas "get to be" suggests opportunity, freedom to become something valued. When one comes right down to it, these two words indicate the difference between one who is saved and one who isn't. To be saved, one has to want to be saved. By definition a true gift is never imposed on an unwilling recipient. One must always be able to accept it or reject it.

Another thing, the gift of God's grace is instantaneous, but the consequences of receiving the gift may be extended over time. This is what I understand Paul to mean when he says in Philippians 3:13, 14: "Brothers, I do not consider myself yet to have taken hold of it. But one thing I do: Forgetting what is behind and straining toward what is ahead, I press on toward the goal to win the prize for which God has called me heavenward in Christ Jesus."

This is also what I take Ellen White to mean when she writes in *Steps to Christ:* "The character is revealed, not by occasional good deeds and occasional misdeeds, but by the tendency of the habitual words and acts" (pp. 57, 58) and in *The Acts of the Apostles:* "So long as Satan reigns, we shall have self to subdue, besetting sins to overcome; so long as life shall last, there will be no stopping place, no point which we can reach and say, I have fully attained. Sanctification is the result of lifelong obedience" (pp. 560, 561).

In summary, what we are saying is that grace is not a substitute for goodness. *Grace is the way to goodness!* We can become the kind of person we truly wish to be. It may take time, perhaps even more time than we have in this life, but we can do it by the grace of our Lord Jesus Christ. Christ is the way.

In the words of Bruce Thielemann:

> Quite frankly, I'm sick to death of ideals. I have so many ideals and I've been so frustrated by them, I really don't care for any more. What I'm looking for is a savior—not someone who will just tell me what I ought to be, but someone who will forgive me for what I am, and then with his very love will enable me to be *more than I ever believed I could be*. It's exactly that that Jesus does ("Telltale Tears," *1986 Preaching Today*, quoted in *Christianity Today*, Oct. 7, 1991, p. 30; italics supplied).

As someone has put it, "Christians are not so much good so they can be saved as they are saved so that they can become good. Salvation becomes credible only as it helps us to achieve goodness." Probably most of us are not as interested in spending eternity with "saved" people as we are in spending it with "good people." But the point is, being "saved" and being "good" are two necessary aspects of one complete whole. This is an essential aspect of the Adventist synthesis. In the next chapter we shall attempt to understand how this is so.

CHAPTER NINE

A New Heart

NOTHING illustrates the power of the Adventist synthesis as clearly as its account of the process by which a sinner may move from death in sin to a life of victory. Here is where our message demonstrates its legitimacy as a prophetic call.

The phrase "progression of truth" implies dependence upon the past but also, as we have suggested, a going beyond it. Those who preceded us, the Reformers, for example, carried the torch as far as they were able. We are in their debt. But there was to be more, and it is in this theological arena that the unique contributions of the Seventh-day Adventist Church, namely the investigative judgment and the heavenly sanctuary, come to bear. (The recent tendency of some to downplay these contributions as at least mildly aberrant represents a far too superficial grasp of their essence.)

Had the Reformers possessed the light given to this people, a *Note* number of their theological formulas, including their forensic (legal) theory of the atonement, might have come out quite differently. What follows is an admittedly tentative attempt to carry the correlation of the past with these "new" insights to its logical conclusion.

Any understanding of the "process" by which human beings are saved, to be adequate, must include four dimensions. If one or more of these is missing, the picture is partial and incomplete. They are:

1. Repentance. Sinners must first *want* to be saved from their sins. This means that they must know that they are sinners, feel genuine sorrow for their sinful state, and choose to do something about it. The decision is theirs alone. Not even God can make it for them. God intervenes in all the ways that the Spirit moves upon the hearts of people, to bring sinners to the point of making the decision. That is, God works to render change a live option. But sinners themselves have to exercise the option.

2. *Forgiveness.* Forgiveness is the fundamental key to the entire process. Everything else we may say about how we are saved is secondary to the statement that God forgives sins and that God alone can do this. Recall the Pharisee's criticism of Jesus for saying to the paralytic, "Friend, your sins are forgiven" (Luke 5:20). They were right. Only God can forgive sins. Their error lay in their failure to recognize that God was in their midst in the person of Jesus.

A prayer for forgiveness is the one prayer that is always answered in the affirmative. God can and does say yes in response to the plea for forgiveness because He is Creator.

The statement "because He is Creator" calls for a bit of elaboration. God's forgiveness is not the same as ordinary human forgiveness. Early in 1984, *Time* magazine recorded an "extraordinary moment of grace."

> In a bare, white-walled cell in Rome's Rebibbia prison, [Pope] John Paul tenderly held the hand that held the gun that was meant to kill him. . . . For 21 minutes, the pope sat with his would-be assassin, Mehmet Ali Agca. The two talked softly. Once or twice, Agca laughed. The pope forgave him for the shooting. At the end of the meeting, Agca either kissed the pope's ring or pressed the pope's hand to his forehead in a Muslim gesture of respect.
>
> It was a startling drama of forgiveness and reconciliation (Jan. 9, 1984, p. 28).

The drama was vitiated somewhat by the pope's entourage. "The only other people in the cell with Agca and John Paul were the pope's personal secretary, two security agents—and a Vatican photographer and television crew." When the pope walked out, Agca was left standing alone. "The camera recorded a sudden look of uncertainty on his face." Was he thinking, *Is that it? Is that all there is?* We have no idea what he expected from the interview.

The pope forgave his would-be assassin, but Mehmet Ali Agca remained, and still remains, in jail—as he ought. Why? Because though forgiven by a fellow human being, even one with enormous prestige and power all around the world, the terrorist in that Roman prison remained *guilty*.

Here is where God's forgiveness differs from human forgiveness. God not only expresses an accepting attitude toward the sinner, as, indeed, the pope did toward Mehmet Ali Agca. *God also removes the guilt.* "It is true that God 'will by no means clear the guilty' (Ex. 34:7), but *He would take away the guilt*" (Ellen G. White, *Thoughts From the Mount of Blessing*, p. 22; italics supplied).

Paul says in Romans 8:1: "Therefore, there is now *no condemnation* for those who are in Christ Jesus." Ellen White tells us, "If you give yourself to Him, and accept Him as your Saviour, then, sinful as your life may have been, for His sake you are accounted righteous. Christ's character stands in place of your character, and you are accepted before God *just as if you had not sinned*" (*Steps to Christ*, p. 62).

God forgives the sin and removes the guilt, and He can do it, and does do it, for repentant sinners because He is the Creator. The new beginning is a new creation, and just as it was at the world's beginning, it is so now because He speaks the new creation into being. Only God can remove both sin and guilt because only God is the Creator. To be made free from guilt is to be given a "clean slate," to be a "new creature." *The new beginning is an act of creation.*

Speaking of becoming perfect, how more perfect can one become than this? And it is available as many times a day as we need it, day after day. The newly created Eden must be dressed and looked after, to be sure. That's where works fit in, but the garden of righteousness is a gift of God free and full. We do not produce it by hoeing weeds in yesterday's "sin-patch."

The fact that we can build our characters on a base of absolute forgiveness rather than on a foundation of guilt provides the possibility of success. That bumper sticker, "Christians are not perfect, they are just forgiven," is mistaken. Christians *are* perfect *just because* they are forgiven—unconditionally. God takes away the guilt, and that perfection which He creates offers the only real opportunity for the developing and perfecting of character—if we will but work at it. But whether or not we live long enough to reach ultimate fulfillment, there is perfection available through forgiveness all along the way as we grow toward becoming the kind of person we truly long to be, "here a little and there a little"—because God is Creator and He forgives our sins. *Grace is not a substitute for goodness, it is the way to achieve it.*

We are the only deficiency in the saving formula: our weak faith. The gift is adequate, if only we can believe it. But there's the rub. As Alfred Korzybski has put it, "God may forgive your sins, but your nervous system won't."

3. *Faith.* The third requirement is thus faith, our faith in His promise. "If we confess our sins, he is faithful and just and will forgive us our sins and purify us from all unrighteousness" (1 John 1:9).

As in repentance, faith involves a choice on our part. Again the choice is made possible by God's gracious assistance. He has given us numerous aids to faith. This was, for example, the function and purpose of the Old Testament sacrificial system. Dispensational notions of God's saving activity are in error. Salvation in the New Testament is the same as it was in the Old, indeed, in whatever age. It is only that there are progressively differing aids to faith appropriate to differing times and places. Salvation was always provided the repentant sinner by the gracious, absolute forgiveness of God.

The sacrificial system was suited to a certain level of understanding and need, but the sacrifice of animals was significant only symbolically. The reality was no different from what it was before the sacrificial system was instituted or after it was abrogated. Human beings have always been saved through God's forgiveness of their sins. There is no other way.

What is required to enable the forgiven sinner to accept the reality is what differs from age to age. When on the ancient Hebrew Day of Atonement the priest, who represented the whole people, carried the blood into the Most Holy Place to present himself before the mercy seat and was accepted there by God, all believing Israelites could receive assurance of God's cleansing. In their representative, the high priest, they were accepted by God.

And as the scapegoat was afterward led out to disappear forever in the wilderness, each could say, "There go my sins." What is important is to note that the ceremony was not directed toward God as manipulative appeasement, as was most often the case in the sacrifices of the surrounding pagans. It was not *necessary* from God's perspective. It was God's way of aiding their faith's acceptance of His free gift.

The same may be said of the heavenly version. The reality is the same, although the manner of its expression is exalted by being placed in the setting of the courts of heaven. Again the high priest represents His people. Another way of translating the Greek term *paraclete*, a word rendered "advocate" in 1 John 2:1 (KJV) or "One who speaks to the Father in our defense" (NIV) and "comforter" in John 15:26 (KJV) or "counselor" (NIV) is "alter ego"—a closer relation than either the KJV or NIV suggests. The Holy Spirit is Christ's "alter ego"—His other self.

Ellen White tells us, "Christ is with us by His Spirit as truly as when, in the days of His humiliation, He moved visibly upon the earth. The lapse of time has wrought no change in His parting promise . . . : 'Lo, I am with you alway, even unto the end of the world' " (*Testimonies*, vol. 4, p. 529). Just as the Holy Spirit is Christ's alter ego, so Christ is our alter ego. We stand before the Father in Him. As the Father deals with Him He deals with us. Our sin, our guilt, has been taken away, and we can believe it because we are accepted by the Father in the person of our alter ego, the heavenly High Priest. (Later we shall explore the implications of Christ's priestly ministry in heaven—1844 and all that.)

There are other aids to faith that instill in us trust and worship. This is the primary task of all theology worthy of the name. And serving others can enhance the sense of personal worth that is the consequence of being accepted by God. Accepting the challenge of the gospel commission to share the good news with our neighbors as well as with the larger world can be a powerful aid to personal faith. Since the essence of sin is distrust and alienation, the sins we commit usually representing maladaptive coping with the underlying problem, that is, fig-leaf garment coverings for our existential nakedness (more of this later. See *Education*, p. 25, and *Christ's Object Lessons*, p. 311.), any relationship or social structure, family or larger community, such as the church, that can help instill a sense of trust and acceptance can function as an aid to faith.

Finally, *4. Divine justice.* It must be demonstrated that God's grace is compatible with His justice, that His forgiveness does not in some way undermine His moral universe. In Paul's words, the actions of the justifier must themselves be justified (Rom. 3:26). The future security of the universe depends upon this being clearly perceived.

In his book *The Prodigal Father* W. Harrington writes:

> We speak glibly of the justice of God. We speak of a *just* God. Well it is for us that our God is *unjust!* We find our hope in the *injustice of God!*
>
> If God be judge, He is the judge who acquits the

guilty—those who enter a plea of "guilty"—while they are yet sinners. It is not a matter of handing down a suspended sentence, or a lenient sentence. No, He simply accepts the plea of "guilty"—and dismisses the case! A human judge who would act so could not hold his job for long. Such conduct is an affront to our idea of justice. But God is doing it all the time (cf. Matt. 18:24-27). We should rejoice in the *injustice* of our God. *We* have a problem in our striving to reconcile God's mercy with His justice. Let us not lose sleep over it: *God* has no such problem. . . . We, too, would do well to welcome the scandal and the foolishness of God's "injustice" (pp. 91-93).

Incredible! Harrington has simply swept away with a cavalier hand a central theme of nearly a millennium of intense theologizing. What does he think all those theories concerning *why* Jesus had to die were about? It has mattered very much to a great many people in this world, and, one suspects, to worlds beyond. The credibility of the kingdom of God and His sovereignty are at issue, and that's not "foolishness." If one cannot depend on the moral verity of God's kingdom, on what can one depend?

Paul often employed legal metaphor in his laying the ground for thinking about why Christ had to die. He gave us no complete theory, although he did greatly influence theories that were to come much later. The so-called forensic, or legal, understanding of the atonement promoted by the major Protestant Reformers, based largely on Paul's language, was designed to deal with this very question, that is, How can God be just and merciful at the same time? Their definition of justice was essentially the old *lex talionis*, an eye for an eye, a tooth for a tooth. (They seemed to have forgotten that Jesus had repudiated this concept of justice in His famous "It hath been said, . . . but I say unto you" exchange [Matt. 5:38, 39, KJV].)

A crime (sin) had been committed, justice demanded that payment be made with a punishment fitting the crime, in this case death, since sin against God is so unthinkable. In mercy God wished to preserve the life of the sinner, the theory went, so He lovingly substituted His own Son, over whom death had no final power.

Roman law, which so greatly conditioned Reformation thinking on this issue, permitted the substitution of an innocent person for the guilty. The principle did not make sense to everyone who heard of it. One of Anselm's (1033-1109) characters in *Cur Deus Homo?* asks in an extended conversation:

> For what justice is there in giving up the most just man of all to death on behalf of the sinner? What man would not be judged worthy of condemnation if he condemned the innocent in order to free the guilty? . . . For if he could not save sinners except by condemning the just, where is his omnipotence? But if he could, but would not, how are we to defend his wisdom and justice? (Anselm of Canterbury, *Cur Deus Homo?* Library of Christian Classics [Philadelphia: Westminster Press, 1956], Vol. X, p. 111. For a more complete treatment of this topic, see the author's *You Can Go Home Again*.).

Some of the rest of us have also wondered how it is that the most unjust thing that ever happened, the crucifixion of our sinless Lord, can satisfy the demands of legal justice. It is an outrage! Surely there must be some other way to reconcile the demands of justice with the mercy of God! Praise God, there is.

But first we need to note that the forensic theory loses much of its force by its dependence upon a faulty Roman principle of law. Present-day jurisprudence recognizes the principle of substitution—in civil law. If I am sued for a civil offense and lose the case, I may not be the one who has to pay. My insurance carrier will probably pick up the tab, thus substituting for me. On the other hand, in a criminal case, no insurance carrier in the land will become responsible. Justice demands that the criminals themselves must pay for their own crimes. (Presumably something worthy of death [sin] is a "crime.") This is why Harrington spoke of the *injustice* of God in allowing the criminal to escape the penalty. However, the legitimate substitutionary role of Christ is found not in faulty jurisprudence. It is found in His being our alter ego in the heavenly sanctuary.

A second thing we must note is that human justice based on the principle of an eye for an eye and a tooth for a tooth, also known as retributive justice, is not the same as divine justice. God satisfies justice on His terms. He suits the punishment to the criminal rather than to the crime. The Eternal Judge, who is by nature merciful, does what is *appropriate* rather than meting out what is *deserved*, and what is appropriate for the truly penitent sinner is forgiveness. The prodigal son belongs home, based not on what he has done but on who and what he is. He was dead but is now alive! The key to this justice is not "an eye for an eye," but to each that which belongs to him, "to each his own."

Enlightened societies have attempted to capture some of God's kind of justice in their punishment of criminals. Inducements to future good behavior or rehabilitation, such as the indeterminate sentence with time off for good behavior, have been tried, only to be discarded. As one warden put it: "Under such a system each inmate automatically becomes a 'con artist,'" trying to demonstrate his eligibility for a reduced sentence, only to return to a life of crime on release.

The problem, of course, is that parole boards can judge only from *outward appearances*. But God is under no such limitation. Only God can accurately judge the heart.

God forgives *repentant* sinners, and it is *just* for Him to do so based on His kind of distributive justice—to each his or her own. It would be *unjust* for Him to forgive *unrepentant* sinners, no matter how skilled they might be at concealing their true intentions. God will not force forgiveness on anyone. He will not and indeed cannot because along with being merciful He is just.

The chief difficulty with God's distributive justice, unfortunately, is that it is easily misunderstood, especially by morally sensitive persons, including those who have never fallen. Harrington's "unjust God" is an example. Salvation of sinners by a just God requires the justification of His act. And here is where the Adventist synthesis has something to say. Those attempts in the past, for example, the forensic theory of the atonement, were heroic attempts to make the jigsaw picture come out whole when there was, in fact, a major piece missing. The "investigative judgment" is precisely that missing part. What might Luther, Calvin, Melanchthon, and the others have done had they only possessed that missing piece of the puzzle! Unfortunately for them, time for that truth had not yet come.

It will be noted that I have resorted to the old-fashioned way of referring to the judgment. "Investigative judgment" is not the same thing as "pre-Advent judgment" and is based on other premises. I am simply rejecting out-of-hand the idea suggested by pre-Advent judgment. There is no pre-advent judgment except in the mind of God, where it is eternal, universal, and rhymes with divine discernment. There is, however, a "judgment" that is already taking place when Christ returns, and this continues during the millennium. I take this to be the meaning of 1 Corinthians 6:2, 3: "Do you not know that the saints will judge the world? . . . Do you not know that we will judge angels?" and Revelation 20:4: "[During the millennium] I saw thrones on which were seated those who had been given authority to judge."

The terms with which we described the investigative judgment in our earlier days seem now somewhat naive in their anthropomorphic literalism now. The essence of the idea need not be, however. The notion that God has to learn something by poring over some books of record is, of course, simple nonsense. The logistics alone are so incredible as to boggle the mind. But the idea that God allows the universe to audit His saving mercy in action, and thus to know that justice was done when forgiveness was granted, is not. It could be that the real subject of the judgment is God Himself. God is on trial in His people. In them the hour of His judgment is come. (C. S. Lewis speaks of *God in the Dock.*)

Whatever are the heavenly symbols or rituals involved on the occasion of the judgment "hour," these are mainly "ant language." The event itself is cosmic in its proportions. That does not eliminate or downplay the literal expression that may be necessary for our comprehension. There may even be a building, and "books"—for our sakes. In the words of John C. Marshall, "all trials are, or should be, 'show trials.' In accordance with the axiom 'Justice must not only be done, but must be seen to be done' " ("The Face of Justice," *Nature,* Feb. 16, 1989, p. 607). As the father takes time to explain things to the older brother in the story of the prodigal, so God allows the universe to behold forgiven sinners as He sees them, to audit His books, and thus He guarantees the future.

When this auditing of the books takes place is a matter that will concern us shortly.

CHAPTER TEN

The Fullness of Time

W E HAVE spoken of God's sanctification of a portion of time (the Sabbath) as a symbol of His creative sovereignty. Time figures prominently in the prophetic movement's message to the world. "The hour [time] of his judgment has come" (Rev. 14:7).

(For much of what immediately follows I am indebted to Alan Richardson, ed., *A Theological Word Book of the Bible*, pp. 258ff.) Several Hebrew and Greek words are translated "time" in our English Bible. Two of these have special relevance to what has been said up to this point. They are the Greek words *chronos* and *kairos*. While these two terms overlap to some extent, there is a significant difference. The distinction is important because it points to a similar same-yet-different quality in God. In this way also time is an appropriate symbol for God.

Chronos is measured time, duration, the passage of time, clock time. Three-thirty in the afternoon is chronological time, as is a short time, a moment, or a long time such as 40 or 1,000 years. *Chronos* is measured by a chronometer—a clock—or a calendar or the phases of the moon and the seasons. *Chronos* expresses continuity.

In contrast, *kairos* is event time, a time of opportunity and fulfillment—what we would mean by "the time is right" or "it's about time." "Now is the time," that is, the conditions or circumstances are right. The whole of history—past, present, and future—consists of times that are all in God's hands. *Kairos* connotes discontinuity. *Kairoi* (plural) may cut across the continuities of history and thus are often extraordinary crisis events by contrast with ordinary, chronological processes. God breaks through into history in *kairoi*. "The hour of his judgment has come" indicates that the *kairos* of the judgment has arrived. Conditions are right for it. The "time" is right.

The time of Jesus was a *kairos*. Jesus affirmed that the expected time had arrived by His words "The time is fulfilled" (Mark 1:15, KJV). The Jews courted disaster by rejecting their opportunity. Christians, by contrast, are discerners of the times and are thus heirs of salvation. Paul says, "They know the seasons" (see Rom. 13:11); "redeem the time" (see Eph. 5:16; Col. 4:5); and "now is the accepted time; . . . behold, now is the day of salvation" (2 Cor. 6:2, KJV). The point is that the "now" in these statements, as *kairos*, is not necessarily 3:00 in the afternoon in the springtime of A.D. 56 or 6:00 p.m., October 22, 1844, for that matter. Both of these may be statements of chronology.

This distinction between *chronos* and *kairos* is an important distinction because there are theologies that, by excessive emphasis on one or the other, fail to take full account of the radical monotheism (wholism) of the Bible and the writings of Ellen White, upon which the essence of the prophetic movement's message so much depends.

God Himself is the aegis of the correlation of these two notions of time when, as Creator and Sustainer of everything that is in the universe, (*Testimonies*, vol. 8, pp. 259, 260), He is at work in the natural, the common, the usual, and the ordinary, as well as in the supernatural, the uncommon, the unusual, and the extraordinary. Natural laws are neither self-operating nor autonomous. They are God's laws, and He continually works through them. God's works can be outlined in science textbooks as readily as they can be transcribed in Holy Scripture. Nature and revelation are not the same thing, but both are qualities of the same unitary reality.

One way to express this is to consider them as two dimensions of that One reality. (The accompanying diagram is an attempt to illustrate the relation.)

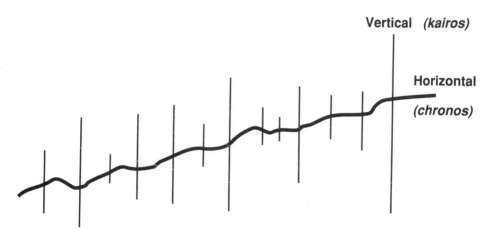

Vertical *(kairos)*

Horizontal

(chronos)

In the above chart the predictable, the repeatable, the continuous, the natural (the scientific), is represented by an ascending horizontal line. (That the line ascends, suggesting progression, is a point that will be explored later.) The unpredictable, the nonrepeatable, the creative, the unique, the personal, the intelligent, is represented by vertical lines transecting the horizontal at certain points. These points of crossing (we speak of "crisis," "crucial," "crux") are moments of "crisis."

The diagram also holds for our distinction between *chronos* and *kairos*. *Chronos* corresponds to the horizontal dimension and *kairos* to the vertical. *Kairoi* cut across the ordinary chronological happenings of life as crisis events. These may be special, even revelatory moments—moments when, for instance, God has broken into history, as in the prophetic encounters of the Bible, the encounter with Israel at Sinai, and especially with the world at the Incarnation. Surely the

Crucifixion was one of the pivotal "crisis" moments of history.

This "crucial" pattern repeats itself at many levels. Human beings, created in God's image, may themselves be defined as a unity of the two transecting dimensions. Human beings share certain continuities as human. These horizontal qualities are physical, material, chemical, anatomic, physiologic in nature. They may be described in terms of substance and process in biological and medical textbooks. They are the subject matter of scientific research and of laboratory investigation. They are shared by all human beings and most of the animals. All people, for example, have blood chemistries that are amazingly similar. Human anatomic variations are minuscule compared with the alikenesses. Even many of our behavioral responses are sufficiently common to us all to enable us to speak of "behavioral sciences."

But human beings are more than just these continuities. There are also vertical discontinuities that distinguish "this particular human being" from all the others. Just as God's "unusual" acts (miracles) are signs of His personality (a major reason for His performing them), so human capacity for free, unique, creative behavior is a mark of human personality. Each individual is not only a well-regulated organism; he or she is also a person. In a well-known passage in her book *Education*, Ellen G. White identifies this quality with the image of God in the human creature.

> Every human being, created in the image of God, is endowed with a power akin to that of the Creator — individuality, power to think and to do. The men in whom this power is developed are the men who bear responsibilities, who are leaders in enterprise, and who influence character. It is the work of true education to develop this power, to train the youth to be thinkers, and not mere reflectors of other men's thought. . . . Instead of educated weaklings, institutions of learning may send

forth men strong to think and to act, men who are masters and not slaves of circumstances, men who possess breadth of mind, clearness of thought, and the courage of their convictions (pp. 17, 18).

This quality is, in fact, the distinguishing feature of humans over against all other creatures. Objects—things—can only be *acted upon*. Living things, plants, and other animals, can also be acted upon, but they may, by contrast with inanimate things, *react*. Such reactions are usually predictable, mainly programmed conditioned responses to stimuli. Human beings share with both nonliving things and living plants and animals their being acted upon and reacting. But the truly human is unique in his or her ability to *act* in ways that are surprising and unpredictable. To be human is not only to be responsive but to be uniquely responsible. It is the mark of personhood.

There are three ways of thinking about humans as "actors." One of them reduces the human to neurons and psychochemistry so that everything an individual does is governed by theoretically explainable mechanisms of cause and effect. "The meaning of the message is to be found in the chemistry of the ink." "Freedom" on this view is mainly an internal illusion one has when one is unaware of all of the causes that affect one. Psychologically, this is the essence of behaviorism. Sometimes it is called somatic reductionism. The self in this mode is reduced to its material, physicochemical organic functions. The corresponding philosophic motif is materialistic humanism. The emphasis is primarily on the horizontal dimension.

A second perspective is that of psychic reduction. In this view the essential self is an immortal, immaterial soul not requiring a body (soma) for conscious existence. The body is temporary and incidental rather than essential to personhood. The corresponding philosophic and theological motif is one in which the vertical dimension is given priority and emphasis. Calvinism and neoorthodoxy, as well as elements of what is being called "new theology" in Adventism, tend to be expressions of this kind of reductionism in theological dress. (We shall say more about this later.)

A third point of view is what we call wholistic. According to this perspective, humans, created in the image of God, are a correlation of both horizontal and vertical dimensions; body and mind, nature and supernature, *chronos* and *kairos*. Just as we may speak of God as a "whole person"—He is One—so we may speak of a human being in whole-person terms, the human and divine each in its own sphere of reality. (Whatever terms such as mind and body may imply when applied to God. It may be useful at this point to review *Testimonies*, vol. 8, pp. 259, 260 on God's relation to nature.)

We pointed out earlier (p. 95) that wholism has long been a central thread in the Adventist synthesis. We have usually expressed it in our understanding of the nature of persons, or, as we formerly put it, "the state of the dead." Ellen White lists "the nonimmortality of the wicked" as one of our relatively few "old landmarks" (*Counsels to Writers and Editors*, p. 30). What has not been so clearly perceived, however, is that this doctrine is about the nature of reality itself. It is in the nature of things that the horizontal and vertical dimensions are both necessary for the whole truth. In the human example, there is no existence of mind apart from a body, and a body without a mind is a "vegetable," we say, and not a functioning person. (We speak of a persistent vegetative state.) The pattern repeats itself again and again. The vertical dimension transects the horizontal, but the two are components of one (wholistic) reality.

Nowhere is this thread more important than in salvation history. It forms the basis for a wholistic understanding of apparent antinomies such as reason and revelation, works and faith, repentance and forgiveness. The cross itself may be so understood. Ellen White tells us:

> Few give thought to the suffering that sin has caused
> our Creator. All heaven suffered in Christ's agony; but

*that suffering did not begin or end with His manifesta-
tion in humanity. The cross is a revelation to our dull
senses of the pain that, from its very inception, sin has
brought to the heart of God* (*Education*, p. 263; italics
supplied).

Revelation 13:8 speaks of "the Lamb that was slain from the
creation of the world." Ever since sin entered the universe God, whose
love and sensitivity are beyond comprehension, has because of that
love been on the cross. Only a rejected, loving parent can even faintly
understand the heart of God during the painful millennia of human
history: the intensity, the duration of it. Listen again to the words of
Ellen White: "Our world is a vast lazar house, a scene of misery that
we dare not allow even our thoughts to dwell upon. Did we realize it
as it is, the burden would be too terrible. Yet *God feels it all*" (*ibid.*,
p. 264; italics supplied).

Again we see the pattern, the horizontal-vertical dimensions.
Those painful millennia constitute the continuity of historic *chronos*.
But at a point in time God pulled back the curtains and revealed what
was always so, in the central *kairos* of the ages. Throughout history a
series of vertical encounters prepared the way for the central event,
and then "when the fulness of the time was come, God sent forth his
Son" (Gal. 4:4, KJV) and "the Word was made flesh, and dwelt among
us, (and we beheld his glory)" (John 1:14, KJV). Since the birth, life,
death, and ascension of our Lord a further series of *kairoi* have
progressively shed light on the central event and will continue to do
so until the crowning event toward which all creation moves.

Adventists have never doubted or denied the centrality of what
took place at the beginning of our era. But, and here is where the
genius of the Adventist synthesis shines through, most of us throughout our history (at least until the furor over *Questions on Doctrine*)
have seen the "Day of Atonement" in terms of something occurring
over a sweep of time rather than being confined to a single, crucial,

legal event no matter how monumental. That sweep had in it important events, including one of greatest significance, but the wholistic pattern runs consistently through the whole. Not only was the Crucifixion event crucial, so is our High Priest's continuing ministry in the heavenly sanctuary.

The essence of the prophetic movement's message in this regard is clear. The original rebellion against God was proposed initially as an attractive alternative to God's way of running things in the universe. God dealt with the rebellion, not by overwhelming it through force, but by allowing it sufficient time to unmask itself. We read in *Patriarchs and Prophets*:

> The true character of the usurper and his real object must be understood by all. He must have time to manifest himself by his wicked works. . . . The whole universe must see the deceiver unmasked. . . . For the good of the entire universe through ceaseless ages, he must more fully develop his principles, that his charges against the divine government might be seen in their true light by all created beings, and that the justice and mercy of God and the immutability of His law might be forever placed beyond question (p. 42).

The horizontal dimension of history is the arena in which the conflict has played itself out. At-one-ment (this is no mere play on words) takes the whole of time (*chronos*) from the original rebellion in heaven until the final consummation and restoration. There are vertical events (*kairoi*) along the way, however, that further the progression of the revelation of the truth about God and His kingdom that is so essential to the reuniting of the separated. (Recall that progression of truth is a fundamental Adventist theme.)

These events may also mark off phases of the progression. The prophetic movement's message for this time is a development, a synthesis of truth that has been long on the way. From the earliest days after the Great Disappointment, Adventists have projected the theme of the Old Testament sanctuary and its primary annual service into the heavens. The earthly Day of Atonement, as is presented in Hebrews, was seen as a model (symbol, or type) of something vastly greater, even cosmic in its scope. It was a discovery of great moment to the little band who survived the Millerite debacle to become a prophetic movement.

The early Adventist vision of Christ's continuing atonement ministry in the highest courts of heaven came virtually to define the movement. Therefore, to be true to our stated objective of preserving our continuities with the past while we change and grow, we must take the concept seriously. (Ellen White certainly did, identifying it with the few "old landmarks" of the movement. See *Counsels to Writers and Editors*, p. 30.) Taking it seriously means that we must learn to recognize the doctrine's essential truth beneath the conceptual clothes that it may be wearing at any particular time. It is that essential truth which must survive. What follows is an attempt to associate those early concepts with paradigms of today.

As we examine the Old Testament type, one of the things we observe is that there is a progression in the ancient atonement ceremony that corresponds to and is shaped by both the tabernacle and later temple structures. The terms "holy place" and "Most Holy Place," applied to the two central compartments, suggest such a progression. But there are other hints. The progression began on Yom Kippur in the surrounding encampment, where the people were gathered for prayer and introspection. Then, moving centrally, the focus shifted to the outer court, where the general populace interfaced with the ordinary priests, leading up to and including their priestly ministry in the secondary of the two main compartments. Finally, there was a movement into the Most Holy Place by the highest order of the priesthood, the high priest himself, and only after special preparation. What we have here is a progression from general, to special, to holy, and then to holiest.

Applying the typical model to its antitype, the cosmic "day" of atonement, we can discern similar patterns of progression. Progression of truth comes readily to mind. The progression of truth begins with general revelation in nature, becomes special revelation in a people and its prophets ("a kingdom of priests"), followed by the disclosure of truth in the incarnation, death, and resurrection of our Lord. This disclosure is further extended by the truths revealed to the New Testament church. And then toward the end of the "day" the heavenly High Priest enters the final phase of His ministry in the Holy of Holies. God proclaims His last-day message to the world. All that remains is the consignment of the Azazel-goat to the wilderness "prison" for 1,000 years, while the redeemed sit in judgment in God's kingdom, the ultimate disclosure. ("Do you not know that the saints will judge the world? . . . Do you not know that we will judge angels?" [1 Cor. 6:2, 3]. "I saw thrones on which were seated those who had been given authority to judge" [Rev. 20:4].)

The earthly type and cosmic antitype are also analogous as they relate to time. Both involve (horizontal) chronological time as well as (vertical) *kairos* time. The Old Testament typical ceremony took time, the better part of a day. This time was punctuated by symbolic events: the gathering of the people; the selection of two unblemished goats; the choice of the goat for God and the one for Azazel; the slaughter of the one chosen for God; the transport of its blood through the holy place to be sprinkled before the mercy seat beyond the veil separating the holy from the Most Holy compartment; and finally the transfer of the guilt-burden to the head of the Azazel-goat, which was then taken out into the wilderness to perish.

The cosmic, antitypical "day" may be seen as covering the entire sweep of chronological history from the Fall to the final restoration. Chronological time is here also punctuated by crisis events (*kairoi*), with God entering history in special ways, such as in the call of

Abraham and a people, the deliverance from Egypt, the law given from Mount Sinai, the epiphanies of the prophets, preeminently the Incarnation and all that it represents, the New Testament church and its gospel to the Gentiles, the call of a people at the end time—the remnant, the second advent of Christ, and the millennium.

These *kairoi* correspond to the various phases of the ancient tabernacle service and structure, and especially with the passage of the High Priest into the Holiest of Holies, the final phase of the "day of at-one-ment." To repeat, the essence of traditional Adventism, rather than concentrating on one, even the main, event by itself, "wholistically" stressed that at-one-ment took time, time punctuated by significant events. This is what we have meant by Christ's continuing ministry on the "day" of atonement. The outer camp, the court, the holy place, and the Most Holy Place progression is a cosmic reality.

The movement of Christ into the heavenly Most Holy Place validated the 1844 expectation for the little band that faithfully stood by. It meant to them that they were not wrong in their time interpretation of Daniel 8:14, only in the place and the nature of the event. It also, by inference, validated their movement. God was with them!

The date 1844, marking the end of the 2300-day/year prophecy, is one of the features of Adventism currently under threat. There is a very real possibility that the movement's continuity with the past may be broken because of this issue, at least for some. I have to admit that I do not find our traditional reading of Daniel's prophecy to be all that unambiguous. There are exegetical problems, and I have heard them forcefully argued about by both sides.

But I do not find this a fact of great importance. We do not need to be entirely clear about what Daniel had in mind when he penned those words. (It would not be the first time that a prophet wrote things that he himself did not understand, or in fact, misunderstood.)

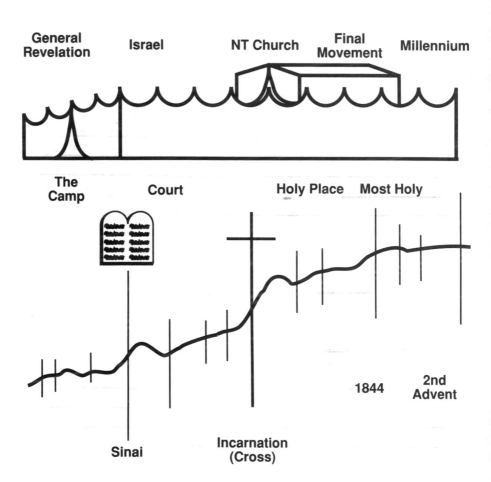

The above is a figure designed to explore at-one-ment as history, the horizontal dimension transected by *karoi*. The Old Testament symbolic Day of Atonement (Yom Kippur) is portrayed as that "day" which takes in the whole of redemption history.

But the point is that our Millerite ancestors and their heirs were convinced from their study that 1843-1844 was the time, and it is more important *what they believed and what they did about it* than what Daniel had in mind. The issue is resolved by history rather than by exegesis! It would also not be the first time that readers and hearers of prophetic messages saw and heard with special eyes and ears. Jesus Himself was able to discern Old Testament references to Himself that are available to us mainly in hindsight. It is difficult to see some things before their time. The year 1844 (perhaps not precisely October 22) was a time of *kairos*. Mid-nineteenth century literally marked the occasion of the beginning of the final separation of the two kingdoms. Of first order importance was the fact that a movement was being born to carry the three-angels' message about God to the world and that the foundation was being laid for the final struggle of the kingdom of light with the kingdom of darkness.

They were mistaken as to what was going to take place at that time. I am not certain that we today know a great deal more about what is taking place in heaven than they did. The usual picture is so out of touch with the literal majesty of the cosmic universe to which we referred earlier—that vast space with those innumerable galaxies and suns—that we can hardly fail to recognize that God is speaking to us in "ant language." Given the present state of our knowledge, it is difficult to believe that the Creator and Sustainer of all that, is saving humankind, as one has put it, "by pushing pots and pans around in a building out there someplace."

Can we know or do we need to know precisely what is going on in heaven? I doubt it. (It is difficult enough to know what is transpiring here on earth without claiming to understand heaven!) It is probably wise for us to let the pictures stand as they are, recognizing them for what they are, celestial metaphors. How else can God tell us the untellable? And of course, symbols, or metaphors, often have objective components.

But what we *can* know is that which has transpired and a measure of what will transpire here on earth. Ellen White makes an interesting comment in *Counsels to Writers and Editors*: "The passing of the time in 1844 was a period of great events, opening to our astonished eyes the cleansing of the sanctuary transpiring in heaven, [and then these words—italics supplied] *and having decided relation to God's people upon the earth*" (*ibid.*). I don't need to know a great deal about what is happening in heaven, but I surely do care about this last phrase.

The announcement that the hour of His judgment has come, and the coincident movement of Christ into the Holy of Holies, could together represent the final phase of the unveiling of God's kingdom. And if it involves the revelation of the truth about God and His judgment hour, then the birth of a movement could figure very prominently in that process. We shall be pursuing this in the next chapter.

CHAPTER ELEVEN

The Fall of Babylon

ANOTHER element in the final prophetic movement's message that clearly expresses its essence is the Adventist interpretation of history. T. S. Eliot recalls encountering Britain's famous, Nobel Prize-winning, skeptical philosopher Bertrand Russell on the street. Author of more than 40 books ranging over philosophy, mathematics, science, ethics, sociology, education, history, religion, and politics, Bertrand Russell was said to be "one of the most widely varied and persistently influential intellects of the twentieth century." Eliot approached the great philosopher with the query, "Lord Russell, what's it all about?" "And you know," Eliot recounted later, "he couldn't tell me."

Adventists have always believed that they knew what was really going on, that they understood the meaning of the play! We have called that understanding the "great controversy between Christ and Satan." It was not an "immaculately conceived" truth, of course. Milton and many others have had a sense for the notion. Indeed, long before there even was a Christian, ancient Zoroastrianism seems to have grasped the controversy's main outlines.

Adventists early on found the concept to be an undercurrent, flowing throughout the entire Bible, although it was largely through the influence of Ellen White's Conflict of the Ages Series, and especially through the last volume in that series, *The Great Controversy*, that it became a key to the three-angels' message.

At the cosmic level the great controversy is an exceedingly

complex concept. So many details are missing in the picture that almost anything we say will be "ant language." "Infinite ideas cannot be perfectly embodied in finite vehicles of thought" (*Selected Messages,* book 1, p. 22). Or in the words of Isaiah, " 'My thoughts are not your thoughts, neither are your ways my ways,' declares the Lord. 'As the heavens are higher than the earth, so are my ways higher than your ways and my thoughts than your thoughts' " (Isa. 55:8, 9).

About all we are going to be able to do at this juncture is to make some crude, impressionistic brushstrokes, to be detailed later when our hands are steadier and our vision clearer. This does not mean that the painting is inaccurate; only incomplete. We shall need the atmosphere of heaven to fill in the specifics. It is important that we try to understand as much as possible now, however, since, to shift the metaphor, we may all be awarded bit parts in the play if we are willing.

To capture this aspect of the Adventist synthesis we must see if we can discover the initial outlines of the controversy. Again, this will not be easy, since we lack detailed information. Anything we say will be to some extent speculative and conjectural. The biblical portrayal of significant numbers of heavenly angels being taken in by Satan's rebellion against God suggests that the temptation was exceedingly subtle. There was little on the surface that suggested anything very "devilish" about it. (We shall have to depend on Spirit of Prophecy sources for most of what immediately follows, since the Bible is largely silent regarding this period, except by way of inference. There are, of course, corroborating texts for most of Mrs. White's key positions if we will but search for them.)

The earthly dimension of the conflict—the temptation of our first parents—is presented in words of Scripture that suggest a theme for the whole.

> Now the serpent was the sliest of all the wild creatures
> that God Yahweh had made. Said he to the woman, "Even
> though God told you not to eat of any tree in the garden

. . ." The woman interrupted the serpent, "But we may eat of the trees in the garden! It is only about the fruit of the tree in the middle of the garden that God did say, 'Do not eat of it or so much as touch it, lest you die!' But the serpent said to the woman, 'You are not going to die. No, God well knows that the moment you eat of it your eyes will be opened and you will be the same as God in telling good from bad' " (Gen. 3:1-5, Anchor).

The "serpent" is a liar, of course. He is "the father of lies" (John 8:44). He should therefore be expected to deny what God had said. But Genesis 3:22 has God Himself saying, "Now that *man has become like one of us* in discerning good from bad, what if he should put out his hand and taste also of the tree of life and eat, and live forever!" (Anchor).

What can this possibly mean? Surely one would think it to be a desirable thing to know good from bad, as God knows good from bad. But here in this passage such knowledge is presented as the original sin against God, resulting in our first parents' banishment from the Garden of Eden.

This mysterious passage refers to something that is appropriate for an attribute of God, but wrong for humans. What can this be? John Greenleaf Whittier says in his poem "The Eternal Goodness": "Not mine to look where cherubim and seraphs may not see, but nothing can be good in Him which evil is in me." But this is not a question of God's existence at a different, and forbidden, level of morality to which mere humans cannot aspire, or perhaps that God is beyond morality, a state inappropriate for His creatures. No, God, as Creator and Sustainer, is the very foundation of morality.

God is self-sufficient in this, as in everything else. Just as He is not dependent on previously existing matter (or energy), so He is not dependent on a moral order or law outside of Himself. All that is necessary for God is that He be self-consistent, by definition.

Just as in His creation of all matter, energy, and ordered biological systems God spoke and it was so, so God alone speaks the moral verities into existence—because He is Creator. Thus for a human to attempt to know good and evil as God knows good and evil is to presume upon a divine prerogative. This is what the "serpent" intended with the invitation to Eve to "be like God." It was an invitation to moral autonomy apart from God, and that is the very essence of sin. Self-sufficiency apart from God is the "original" sin. A variety of humanisms and situationisms formally express this quality of moral autonomy today. Human autonomy and self-sufficiency apart from God versus trustful dependence on God constitute the two sides in the great controversy.

Ellen G. White describes the conflict in terms of disobedience or obedience to God's law.

> The warfare against God's law, which was begun in heaven, will be continued until the end of time. Every man will be tested. Obedience or disobedience is the question to be decided by the whole world. All will be called to choose between the law of God and the laws of men. Here the dividing line will be drawn. There will be but two classes. Every character will be fully developed; and all will show whether they have chosen the side of loyalty or that of rebellion.

> Then the end will come. God will vindicate His law and deliver His people (*The Desire of Ages*, p. 763).

The controversy can be identified as two competing notions of freedom. We read:

> The law of love being the foundation of the government of God, the happiness of all created beings depended upon their perfect accord with its great principles of righteousness. God desires from all His creatures the service of love—homage that springs from an intelligent

appreciation of His character. He takes no pleasure in a forced allegiance, and to all He grants freedom of will, that they may render Him voluntary service.

But there was one that chose to pervert this freedom (*The Great Controversy*, p. 493).

God's adversary is often depicted in destructive terms which suggest that Satan's whole purpose was to tear down every good thing that came from God. The evidence implies, however, that what Satan was offering was an alternative to God's way, an appealing alternative in many respects. "Satan claimed to be able to present laws which were better than God's statutes and judgments" (*Selected Messages*, book 1, p. 316).

He began to insinuate doubts concerning the laws that govern heavenly beings, intimating that though laws might be necessary for the inhabitants of the worlds, angels, being more exalted, needed no such restraint, for their own wisdom was a sufficient guide. They were not beings that could bring dishonor to God; all their thoughts were holy; it was no more possible for them than for God Himself to err. . . . It was his object to secure freedom for all (*Patriarchs and Prophets*, p. 37).

He promised those who would enter his ranks a new and better government, under which all would enjoy freedom (*ibid.*, p. 40).

It was apparently a novel suggestion. In the harmony of heaven the angels had not even thought of law and obedience or of the need for more freedom.

When Satan rebelled against the law of Jehovah, the thought that there was a law came to the angels almost as an awakening to something unthought of. In their ministry the angels are not as servants, but as sons. . . . Obedience is to them no drudgery. Love for God makes their service a joy (*Thoughts From the Mount of Blessing*, p. 109).

The problems raised by Satan's and his followers' disaffection are dealt with by God mainly by revealing the truth about the two alternatives—God's way as over against the way of self-sufficiency apart from God. There must also be sufficient time allowed to make an adequate disclosure. In the words of Ellen White:

> The true character of the usurper and his real object must be understood by all. He must have time to manifest himself by his wicked works. . . . His own work must condemn him. . . . The whole universe must see the deceiver unmasked. . . . For the good of the entire universe through ceaseless ages, he must more fully develop his principles (*Patriarchs and Prophets*, p. 42).

> Until fully developed, it could not be made to appear the evil thing it was; his disaffection would not be seen to be rebellion. Even the loyal angels could not fully discern his character or see to what his work was leading (*ibid.*, p. 41).

What we are looking for behind the mask is the true nature of Satan's alternative and its consequences. That is what the great controversy is all about. The full consequences are known to us only by predictive prophecy, since they remain yet future. But enough has been revealed in the world already to give us some understanding of the second and third angels' dire pronouncements.

As to those who belong to God's kingdom the picture is clear. They are those "who obey God's commandments and remain faithful to Jesus" (Rev. 14:12). "There is perfect unity between them and their Creator. Obedience is to them no drudgery. Love for God makes their service a joy. So in every soul wherein Christ, the hope of glory, dwells, His words are re-echoed, 'I delight to do thy will, O my God: yea, thy law is within my heart' (Ps. 40:8)" (*Thoughts From the Mount of Blessing*, p. 109). Their future is eternal life in the kingdom of God. There, in trustful, creative dependence, "they follow the Lamb wherever he goes" (Rev. 14:4), and they are characterized by trustful, creative dependence on God even now.

More must be said about the nature and future of the alternative kingdom. We noted earlier that the issue was freedom, freedom that is the result of complete trust in God versus freedom that is based on autonomy apart from God—"doing one's own thing." Absolute autonomy and true freedom are, in fact, a contradiction in terms, even if there were only one person on earth. A solitary individual would find competing drives and desires in tension with each other within his or her breast. Where there is more than one individual, the freedom of each will be in competition. The greater the number of people involved, the less individual freedom there can be—if there is to be any kind of order. Individual freedoms often have to be surrendered in favor of social order. Certainly one couldn't run an airline, a railroad, or a highway traffic system on the basis of absolute autonomy.

Absolute autonomy inevitably leads to tyranny. As individual freedoms compete for power, a struggle for dominance develops in which those with the greatest strength, power, ability, (or weaponry) climb to the top of the heap. The big fishes eat the little fishes, and the little fishes eat the littler fishes in a continuing struggle for survival. In the end the "fittest," in the sense of those more powerful, survive and become tyrants over the weaker and "unfit." Ellen White says of Satan, "He had claimed that the transgression of God's law would bring liberty and exaltation; but it was seen to result in bondage and degradation" (*The Great Controversy*, p. 502).

This alternative, each doing his or her own thing, looking after his or her own interests, is the way things largely are in the natural and social world as we now know it. The big fishes *do* eat the little fishes, and the little fishes *do* eat the littler fishes in the seas and on Wall Street, and mostly it seems to work rather well. There is a balance in nature, for example, that, unless it is upset by major or minor catastrophes such as mankind can bring, does fairly evenly maintain itself. Indeed, when all the predators disappear from nature, things go grossly awry. When you don't have the big fishes around, or even enough little fishes, you may end up with too many littler fishes. Capitalistic business enterprise does produce a higher standard of living than other systems, at least for those who are able to benefit from it. If the titans of the free enterprise system go under, the poor face starvation. Satan's survival-of-the-fittest system appears to work—in the short run.

But the great controversy is about the long run. What appears to succeed in some respects has within it the seeds of its own dissolution. That truth must out. Satan's kingdom has come so to dominate the world that it is often difficult to distinguish in nature and the present social order any other kind of possibility. It is there, if one has eyes to see it. Nature—both human and the rest—still testifies to its Creator. But it is a mixed testimony. This is one of the reasons that "naturalistic" moral systems prove to be so unsatisfactory. If one attempts to determine moral behavior by looking at the way things take place in nature—that is, as the moral philosophers say, to determine the *ought* from the *is*—one runs squarely into the fact that what *is* is not always the way things *ought* to be.

And how do we know that? We know it because God is supporting His side of the great controversy and will continue to support it until the inevitable victory. One of the ways He supports it is by His self-disclosure. We know how we ought to behave because we know what kind of God He has revealed and is revealing Himself to be. We also know it because He has told us how that which He has created ought to behave when it is true to itself.

Note the future ideal ecosystem suggested by the prophet Isaiah in chapter 65. (I am aware of the poetic imagery in these verses. The choice of such imagery is, however, not without significance.)

"Behold, I will create new heavens and a new earth" (verse 17). "The wolf and the lamb will feed together, and the lion will eat straw like the ox. They will neither harm nor destroy on all my holy mountain" (verse 25).

Jesus made the same point in His depiction of the ideal *ego*-system when He responded to His disciples' persistent conflict over who was going to be "on the top of the heap" in His kingdom.

> You know that the rulers of the Gentiles lord it over them, and their high officials exercise authority over them. Not so with you. Instead, whoever wants to be great among you must be your servant, and whoever wants to be first must be your slave—just as the Son of Man did not come to be served, but to serve, and to give his life a ransom for many (Matt. 20:25-28).

Never was the essential contrast of the two kingdoms more clearly epitomized than in the words—and life—of this God-man who dwelt among us. God's kingdom knows nothing of predation, either at the natural or human-social level. And that makes all the difference. The contrast between them is revealed in the ultimate consequences of the two freedoms. Freedom as self-sufficiency leads to tyranny and self-destruction. Freedom under God leads to eternal life.

CHAPTER TWELVE

Come, Let Us Build a Tower

THE tangled skein of the demonic competitive struggle between self-serving dominance and self-sacrificing love, which has characterized the world through the ages, will, according to the Bible, one day be separated out so all can see the difference between the two kingdoms in sharpest contrast.

In Jesus' parables about the sheep and goats and the wheat and tares, the separation will take place at the end of the world, and He admonished His followers not to attempt the separation before the time lest good wheat be lost.

But the day would surely come. Indeed, that day of final polarization has been the end-point toward which the conflict of the ages has been steadily pointing. This is what constitutes the "finishing of the work," which Adventists have anticipated rather than the geographics and demographics of knocking on all the doors of earth with the 27 doctrines. And this is also the reason that it is so difficult to tell the day or the hour of our Lord's appearing.

Geographics and demographics are quantifiable. It is theoretically possible to know when all the doors have been knocked on. It is not possible to know about the adequacy of the disclosure of the truth about the two kingdoms—unless, of course, you are God. At issue is the character of God and of Satan, and thus the issue is of cosmic proportions. It is not merely a question of individual salvation, as important as that is to each saved or lost person. Ultimately God is on trial, and we may be far closer to the conclusion of that trial than any one of us has imagined!

It is possible, however, to watch the controversy intensify and build toward that climax. In the latter part of the nineteenth century there lived a philosopher who, based on his impact on human life on this planet, can plausibly be called one of the most influential thinkers of modern times. Born in Prussia in the year 1844, Friedrich Nietzsche was reared mainly by his mother and sister in a somewhat straitlaced Lutheran home. His father, a Lutheran pastor, died when Friedrich was 5. Friedrich rebelled against Christianity at the age of 18, saying later that it was the easiest thing he ever did. He was to spend much of the rest of his life trying to prove it was the easiest thing he ever did! In 1888, after a brilliant life of letters, he wrote, as major evidence for this, *Der Antichrist*, a scathing diatribe against Christianity and all it stands for. No one could have projected more forcefully the ethos of the demonic kingdom. But let him speak for himself:

> What is good? Everything that heightens the feeling of power in man, the will to power, power itself. What is bad? Everything that is born of weakness. What is happiness? The feeling that power is growing, that resistance is overcome. Not contentedness but more power; not peace but war; not virtue but fitness. . . . What is more harmful than any vice? Active pity for all the failures and all the weak: Christianity. . . . What type of man shall be bred, shall be willed, for being higher in value, worthier of life, more certain of a future? . . . Christianity should not be beautified and embellished. It has waged deadly war against this higher type of man; it has placed all the basic instincts of this type under the ban; and out of these instincts it has distilled evil and the

Evil One (Walter Kaufmann, *The Portable Nietzsche*, pp. 570ff.).

Nietzsche said that Christian theologians had stood morality on its head by justifying weakness, as in "blessed are the meek." The truly noble ones in Christ's day were the Roman soldiers who marched through the world conquering weakness and decadence. They were the supermen of their time. It should be obvious that such ideas were founded on another modern intellectual revolution, one associated with the name of Charles Darwin. Nietzsche's viewpoint was a powerful expression of social Darwinism.

Darwin's *Origin of Species*, published in 1859, is without question one of the most influential books ever written. In 1842 Darwin prepared a 48-page "sketch" of the theory of natural selection. Then in 1844, the year of Friedrich Nietzsche's birth, he produced an essay (which was, in fact, very much a finished book) presenting the theory in greater detail. Darwin did not relish the controversy that he was sure would accompany formal publication of his ideas, especially as it would be interpreted as an attack on Christianity. As a consequence, he delayed publication of *Origin* until he was virtually forced to do so. This larger book, for which he is mainly remembered, added little real substance to the 1844 essay.

As is true with virtually all human ideas, Charles Darwin's theory was also not "immaculately conceived." There were many others at the time and before him whose thoughts were moving in that direction. He did provide key elements to the idea, however, that gave it a certain cogency and, very quickly, general acceptance.

Few thought-forms have affected intellectual life on this planet as profoundly as has the general theory of evolution, the formulation of which depended so heavily on Charles Darwin. One of Darwin's chief impacts was social.

For most of preceding history the relation of humanity to nature was one in which men and women were something special—specially created and specially endowed. Humankind bore the image of God. For the Darwinians, by contrast, human beings are simply part of nature, subject to its origins, laws, and destiny.

This meant that the natural struggle for survival and dominance— the big fishes eating the little fishes, the law of fang and claw—applies also to human society. Among people, too, the "fittest" survive. At least this is the direction Friedrich Nietzsche and his friends were wont to go. Marx and Engels were delighted with Darwin's theoretical support for their dialectical materialism and tried to persuade Darwin to allow his name to appear in the dedication of *Das Kapital*. It was, to his credit, an invitation that he politely refused.

Motivated and informed by Darwin, Nietzsche's social impact was chiefly felt in his *Der Antichrist* (*The Antichrist*) and *Der Wille zur Macht* (*The Will to Power*). (The titles identify the kingdom to which these works belong.)

The basis for the statement that Nietzsche had had so profound an influence on the modern world is the fact that (it is said) "Adolf Hitler slept with Friedrich Nietzsche under his pillow." *Mein Kampf* is liberally laced with passages straight from the pen of Nietzsche. It would be naive to suggest that the two world war disasters of our century were fathered by the writings of one man, be he ever so forceful, but Nietzsche was surely their philosophic "soul-mother." And he came close to hovering over a third and unimaginably terrible war owing to the fact that Darwinism was introduced promptly into Leninist and Stalinist Russia, where it was received with great enthusiasm. (See Philip T. Grier, "Something New Under the Tsars," *Science*, August 1989, p. 769.)

Note the sentiments of Nietzsche in a perceptive article entitled "Biological Science and the Roots of Nazism," by George J. Stein, published in *American Scientist*, January-February 1988, pp. 50ff.

A people that interferes with natural selection
through permitting anyone to breed merely introduces

even larger numbers of the less fit into the population pool. This "mockery of Nature and her will" must lead to disaster. A nation which has not followed natural selection in developing its population will "some day be deprived of existence on this earth; for man can defy the eternal laws of the will to conservation for a certain time, but sooner or later vengeance comes. . . . A stronger race will drive out the weak, for the vital urge in its ultimate form will, time and time again, burst all the absurd fetters of the so-called humanity of individuals, in order to replace it by the humanity of Nature which destroys the weak to give his place to the strong." . . . In the end, Nature asserts herself, and "only the urge to self-preservation will avail." Thus, the infamous phrase: "Mankind has grown great in eternal struggle, and only in eternal peace does it perish." . . . War [is] justified as the natural right of any breeding community taking what is needed for survival. "We must, therefore, coolly and objectively adopt the standpoint that it is certainly not the intention of Heaven to give one people fifty times as much land and soil in this world as another. . . . We must not let political boundaries obscure the boundaries of eternal justice." . . . And if the other will not share the earth willingly, "then the law of self-preservation goes into effect" and Germany will take what it needs. (The above are all quotations from Hitler's *Mein Kampf.*)

Social Darwinism, mediated through Nietzsche's *The Antichrist*, is very clearly the undercurrent of a speech Der Führer made before his generals just prior to the invasion of Poland.

Close your hearts to pity! Act brutally! Eighty million people must obtain what is their right. . . . Be hard and remorseless! Be steeled against all signs of compassion!

. . . Whoever has pondered over this world order knows
that its meaning lies in the success of the best by means
of force (William L. Shirer, *The Nightmare Years*, p.
427).

A generation earlier, Kaiser Wilhelm II had expressed sentiments
similar to Adolf Hitler's. Speaking of his nation, he declared, "No one
can dispute with us the place in the sun that is our due" (quoted in
Time, July 3, 1989, p. 48). (Incidentally, Chairman Mao Tse-tung
regarded Darwin, as presented by the German Darwinists, to be the
foundation of Chinese scientific socialism. See George Stein, p. 52.)

The above is pursued at such length in order to give support to the
contention that something of great significance to the great controversy between Christ and Satan was taking place here on earth around
the middle of the nineteenth century. The precise date—1844—may
be incidental, but it is at least interesting that the completion of
Charles Darwin's major essay; the birth of the philosophic father of
social Darwinism, Friedrich Nietzsche; and the call of an American
movement to be an instrument in the hands of God to finish His work
all took place in that year. (It was a vintage year!)

All this took place against the backdrop of the Industrial Revolution, which was destined to bring the world into contact and
interaction through communications and travel in a manner un-
equaled during the history of humanity.

We may not know what literally took place in heaven in 1844, but
it is undeniable that there was great plenty taking place here on earth.
It would surely seem plausible to look at these events as an occasion
of heavenly *kairos*. It does not seem unwarranted to refer to the birth
of a movement in such a setting as coterminous with the passage of
Christ into the Holy of Holies in heaven, the final progression of
earth's "day" of at-one-ment.

Could it be that in mid-nineteenth century there began the last
phase of the divine self-disclosure, along with the ultimate demon-

stration of the kingdom of darkness, sharply exposing the essential nature of the two kingdoms and calling the whole world, indeed the whole universe, into final judgment in that revelation? In that judgment the true nature of the kingdom of God with its harmony of order, trust, love, and justice is clearly contrasted with the false claims of the kingdom of darkness. Satan's kingdom, which at its beginning seemed so appealing and innocuous, is at the end shown to be what it truly is for all to see, and the future is secured.

It is appropriate that the two kingdoms should be called the remnant and Babylon in the final stages of their warfare. Adventists have thought of themselves as that remnant from the movement's earliest beginnings. (The analogy was drawn from what remains of a bolt of cloth after everything really large enough to make anything is used up. As a boy I used to wonder about the connotation of "leftovers"—as in "supper"—an expression not always accompanied by the pleasantest of associations in our relatively impoverished home.)

Remnant is a somewhat technical word, occurring with some frequency in Scripture, usually suggesting the idea of God's "true" people. "I will surely gather all of you, O Jacob; I will surely bring together the remnant of Israel" (Micah 2:12). The final remnant of Revelation 12:17 indicates those who "remain" faithful, that is, as in "be thou faithful unto death" (Rev. 2:10, KJV) in the face of the fury of the dragon. It is a term that has special relevance at the very end of the conflict.

There is a sense, however, in which the expression may be applied to the remnant before that final moment. Theologians use a special noun—prolepsis. The adjective proleptic can mean "present by anticipation" or "the representation or assumption of a future act or development as being presently existing or accomplished." For example, the resurrection of Jesus is proleptic of the general resurrection of all the faithful, the firstfruits anticipating and representing the full harvest.

It is the name Babylon in the book of Revelation that intrigues us most. A cryptonym for Rome? Probably. It was undoubtedly prudent to avoid using the official name in connection with such writings in the last part of the first century, especially by one who was already banished for his faith. The church would understand. But why Babylon? There is no evidence that these prophetic messages had any connection with the Babylon of Mesopotamia in the first or any other century for that matter. No. The name identifies a power that would wage war against the remnant of God in the last days, a power symbolized (in the Tillichian sense) by that ancient city with its tower ascending into the heavens (Gen. 11:3-9). The Tower of Babel was so named because of the confusing of tongues that stopped its building. (The word Babel sounds similar to the Hebrew word meaning confused.) But its use as the name for the power seeking to destroy the remnant who keep the commandments of God was far more significant than anything that ancient story suggests on the surface.

For what does that ancient city with its tower stand? In a perceptive article in *American Scholar*, Leon R. Kass, M.D., professor in the College and the Committee on Social Thought at the University of Chicago, recounts the ancient tale of the Tower of Babel and applies it to our day. In the process he has captured the essence of "Babylon" as the kingdom of Satan in every age, including our own.

> The building of the city and tower is an expression of powerful human impulses, at first toward safety and permanence, eventually toward full independence and self-sufficiency, and accomplished entirely by rational and peaceful means: by forethought and planning, by arts to transform the given world, and by cooperative social arrangements made possible by common speech and uniform thoughts. This ancient story encapsulates a

recurrent human dream of universal human community living in peace and freedom, no longer at the mercy of an inhospitable or hostile nature, and enjoying a life no longer solitary, nasty, poor, brutish, and short. The universal city is the bearer and embodiment of this dream. . . .

First is the condition of simple innocence in the Garden of Eden. Innocence is destroyed when man, his desires enlarged by newly used powers of mind, exercises his autonomy and takes to himself independent knowledge of good and bad; judgmentally self-conscious, he immediately discovers his nakedness, and thus his shame and wounded pride, which he artfully attempts to clothe over. . . .

After the Flood, God promised "Never again," but it is reasonable to surmise that the memory of the Deluge weighed at least as heavily as the hearsay report of God's promise not to repeat it. . . . If what lies behind the human world is only chaos and instability, man must make his own order. *Human ordering is the theme of Babel* (Winter 1989, pp. 41ff; italics supplied).

The city is a mixture of pride and fear. . . . Having (at best) hearsay knowledge of God's promise to Noah ("No more floods," no total destruction), these men are inclined rather to trust to self-help for protection against the state of nature and the wide open spaces. . . . Beginnings in fear gradually give rise to pride. . . . The city and tower express the human conquest of necessity, human self-sufficiency and independence. . . . The aspiration to reach heaven is in fact a desire to bring heaven into town, either to control it, or more radically, to efface altogether the distinction between the human and the natural or divine. In the end men will revere nothing and will look up to nothing not of their own making, to nothing beyond or outside of themselves. . . .

The project of Babel has been making a comeback. . . . Science and technology are again on the make, defying political boundaries en route to a projected Human Empire over nature. . . .

The city is back, and so, too, is Sidom [*sic*], babbling and dissipating away. Perhaps we ought to see the dream of Babel today, once again, from God's point of view (*ibid.*).

It is hard to imagine a more graphic picture of what is foretold in Revelation. But, we want to know, what is it that brings about the separation, the polarization of the two kingdoms at the end? Let me hazard a suggestion, essentially the same sort of thing that set the stage for Babel of old. *They didn't believe the rainbow of promise*, and if you cannot trust God, you are on your own! This has been the story from the beginning of time. Separation from and distrust of God has led to guilt and anxiety, which has resulted in human's making attempts to achieve security and feelings of worth and power by their own individual and institutional works. Fig leaves come in all colors, sizes, and shapes.

There you have it! The essence of the conflict through the ages has been salvation by faith in God versus salvation by human works—the garden temptation, the sacrifices of Cain and Abel, ancient Babel, the failures of Israel, clear on down to "Babylon" and the final war at the end—trustful, responsible dependence upon God versus human self-sufficiency and autonomy apart from God—and the consequences of each. As they say, that's what it is all about.

Being able to keep track of the final developments, for instance, the creation of the powerful, coercive force that wages final war against the remnant—one of the traditional interest themes of the

Adventist movement—depends upon a certain perceptivity regarding the roots of such behavior. Surrender to authoritarian control is often the mark of uncertainty and insecurity. Stephen M. Sales tells us that

> psychoanalysts have long maintained that threat evokes a characteristic pattern of defenses. When we are afraid, they say, we turn to strong leaders who can protect us. We become intolerant of outgroups and of those who differ from us. We admire power and those who wield power, we come to despise weakness and ambiguity, and we become superstitious. In short, we become authoritarian ("Authoritarianism," *Psychology Today*, November 1972, p. 94).

Sales states that churches that are authoritarian do better in bad times than in good. He even found it possible to correlate the popularity of strong "masculine" (authoritarian) comic strips inversely with the economic and political health of the country. William Irwin Thompson, writing in *Quest*, says that people who are frightened, angry, and out of work will easily surrender their civil liberties to an authoritarian and paternalistic state if it will only take care of them (May/June 1977, p. 92).

A long time ago Fyodor Dostoyevsky had his grand inquisitor say:

> And we alone shall feed them in Thy name, declaring falsely that it is in Thy name. Oh, never can they feed themselves without us! No science will give them bread so long as they remain free. In the end they will lay their freedom at our feet, and say to us, "Make us your slaves but feed us." . . . I tell thee that man is tormented by no greater anxiety than to find someone quickly to whom he can hand over that gift of freedom with which the ill-fated creature is born. But only one who can appease their conscience can take over their freedom (*The Broth-*

ers Karamazov, Trans. by Constance Garnett, pp. 300-302).

Adolf Hitler rode to power on the political and economic shambles of post-World War I Germany. All we need is a period of deep and prolonged socioeconomic disaster and it could happen again.

In a book about which every Seventh-day Adventist should know, Robert L. Heilbroner (at the time of writing he was Norman Thomas Professor of Economics at the New School for Social Research in New York) lays bare precisely those roots:

> There is a question in the air, more sensed than seen, like the invisible approach of a distant storm, a question I would hesitate to ask aloud did I not believe it existed unvoiced in the minds of many: "Is there hope for man?" . . .
>
> The question asks whether we can imagine that future other than as a continuation of the darkness, cruelty, and disorder of the past; worse, whether we do not foresee in the human prospect a deterioration of things, even an impending catastrophe of fearful dimensions. . . .
>
> The outlook for man, I believe, is painful, difficult, perhaps desperate, and the hope to be very slim indeed. . . . The answer to whether we can conceive of the future other than as a continuation of the darkness, cruelty, and disorder of the past seems to me to be no; and to the question of whether worse impends, yes (*An Inquiry Into the Human Prospect*, pp. 13-22).

For the next 122 pages Professor Heilbroner reviews the clouds that threaten our common sky: social evils, drugs, street crime, sexual irresponsibility, the despoiling of our environment with resulting serious climatic changes, overpopulation with an ever more reduced standard of living, wars of redistribution and/or of presumptive seizure in the face of an ever-diminishing supply of natural resources. He speaks darkly of "an immense train, in which a few passengers, mainly in the advanced capitalist world, ride in first-class day coaches, in conditions, unimaginable to the enormously greater numbers crammed into the cattle cars that make up the bulk of the train's carriage" and of the possibility that those masses may one day make use of the horror weapons of the twentieth century to blackmail the first-class passengers into dividing up their creature comforts.

In contemplating what it would require to head off our certain rendezvous with disaster, Dr. Heilbroner sees only a very radically altered political situation.

> The eventual rise of "iron" governments, probably of a military-socialist cast, seems part of the prospect that must be faced (*ibid.*, p. 39).

> Candor compels me to suggest that the passage through the gauntlet ahead may be possible only under governments capable of rallying obedience far more effectively than would be possible in a democratic setting. If the issue for mankind is survival, such governments may be unavoidable, even necessary (*ibid.*, p. 110).

> From that period of harsh adjustment, I can see no realistic escape. . . . If then, by the question "Is there hope for man?" we ask whether it is possible to meet the challenges of the future without the payment of a fearful price, the answer must be: No, there is no such hope (*ibid.*, p. 136).

Professor Heilbroner gives us in the above about as good a description of the events depicted in Revelation 13 as could be expected from one unfamiliar with the Bible.

All this should have a familiar ring to Adventists, at least to older church members, who remember the evangelistic preaching of former days. It may seem a bit unrealistic to some younger believers, who have become accustomed to hearing about a "far-off divine event" that is unlikely to affect them unduly in the fairly comfortable present. Many of us, at least in the First World, have come to expect our first-class tickets. It is easy with the passage of time for belief to become believing in believing, and because of this the question of when still hangs—or should hang—heavily on the air. That is also an essential part of the Adventist prophetic movement's message. We will have some things to say about that in our next and final chapter.

CHAPTER THIRTEEN

The Right People, the Right Places, and the Right Time

TRADITIONAL Adventism has expected the faithful in heart in the world, even in the "fallen churches," to come out at the end from wherever they are ("Come out of her, my people" [Rev. 18:4]) to join the remnant (the Adventist) church in its opposition to Babylon. Ellen G. White set the pattern early on:

I saw that God has honest children among . . . the fallen churches, and before the plagues shall be poured out, ministers and people will be called out from these churches and will gladly receive the truth. Satan knows this, and before the loud cry of the third angel is given he raises an excitement in these religious bodies, that those who have rejected the truth may think God is with them. He hopes to deceive the honest and lead them to think that God is still working for the churches. But the light will shine, and all who are honest will leave the fallen churches, and take their stand with the remnant (*Early Writings*, p. 261).

Later she would write:

In . . . Africa, in the Catholic lands of Europe and of South America, in China, in India, in the islands of the sea, and in all the dark corners of earth, God has in reserve a firmament of chosen ones that will yet shine forth amidst the darkness, revealing clearly to an apostate world the transforming power of obedience to His law. Even now they are appearing in every nation, among every tongue and people; and in the hour of deepest apostasy . . . these faithful ones . . . will "shine as lights in the world." The darker the night, the more brilliantly will they shine (*Evangelism*, pp. 706, 707).

Then thousands in the eleventh hour will see and acknowledge the truth. . . . These conversions to truth will be made with a rapidity that will surprise the church, and God's name alone will be glorified (*Selected Messages*, book 2, p. 16).

A number of quinquennia ago, when the General Conference was in session in Vienna, Austria, newly reelected General Conference president Robert Pierson was interviewed by a non-Adventist reporter from *Christianity Today*. The interview, later published, contained the following exchange:

Q. What do you mean when you speak of "God's remnant church"?

A. We believe, from our reading of the book of Revelation and other parts of Scripture, that today God has a remnant church, the last before the coming of Jesus. Seventh-day Adventists do not teach that only they will be saved. God's people are in all churches. We believe that before Jesus returns many will respond and join the remnant church.

Q. Does this mean that they will join the Adventist Church?

A. We believe that our message will call many of them to join us in preparation for the coming of Christ (Aug. 29, 1975, p. 42).

It was a legitimate question. The reporter was probably not comfortable with some of the things he had heard at the meetings.

References to "God's true church," "God's people," and the like undoubtedly sounded to his *Christianity Today* ears as displaying more than a little sectarian arrogance.

But what if the final remnant is mainly a quality of life and faith rather than an established institution? Could it be that, when the final polarization of the two kingdoms takes place, there will be insufficient time—or need—to warrant shaping the "gathering" into a formally organized megachurch? "The final movements will be rapid ones." The Babylon that remains, rejected by God and abandoned by His faithful people, will quickly self-destruct unless God intervenes. *Unmixed evil has a very short half-life.* (There has to be a measure of goodness, at least some honor, even among thieves, or no thieves would survive. It is only because of the good wheat in the field that the tares are allowed to persist until the harvest.) Unfortunately, unmixed evil is not only self-destructive, it attempts to destroy every good thing within its reach. This is the reason that the hand of God must also intervene to protect His people at the end.

What is being suggested is that the final remnant gathering may be broader and more extensive than any formal church, as such, can possibly organize, however successful its proselytizing strategies. This is said while giving full credit to the proleptic use of the term "remnant."

What, then, beside prolepsis, is the relation of the prophetic movement to the remnant? If what is implied above is correct, the movement may, at the very last, lose itself in something bigger than itself, in the way that John the Baptist—the Elijah of his day—experienced a diminution of his own influence while that of his Lord increased. The proleptic remnant may one day be absorbed into the final remnant that it has played such an important part in bringing into being.

Meanwhile, during the days of preparation, the movement—if true to its calling—will be an instrument of truth in God's hand, giving unmistakable testimony regarding the character of their King and of His kingdom. In the words of Ellen White:

> At this time a message from God is to be proclaimed, a message illuminating in its influence and saving in its power. His character is to be made known. Into the darkness of the world is to be shed the light of His glory, the light of His goodness, mercy, and truth (*Christ's Object Lessons*, p. 415).

Here is theology at its best, theology in the sense of knowing God and making Him known. And, of course, knowing Him is more than a set of abstract theological formulas about Him. So is making Him known more than distributing verbal pronouncements. The prophetic movement is called to *be* as well as to *say*. They are to be a light set on a hill, the salt of the earth, the leaven in the lump. God is to be revealed *in* as well as *by* His called people!

But again, a question we asked at the outset: How can so small a drop of water affect so large a bucket of change? It seems almost a prerequisite of prophets that they feel inadequate in the face of their assigned tasks. Elijah of old fled into the wilderness after the contest on Mount Carmel. He felt deeply depressed and alone. He wished to die. Until God assured him that thousands in Israel had not bowed their knees to Baal. He could wonder where they were when he needed them, but God knew. They were there. (Can those bearing the Elijah message for the end time expect any less?) They were there and they came out when the time was right. The proleptic role must first be played out.

The anticipatory role of the prophetic movement in the final polarization may be illustrated by a fact of elementary physics. It is possible to cool water to below its freezing point without its freezing. The water should be free of impurities—preferably distilled—and one must handle it with some care. But it can be done. However, super-cooled water is very unstable. All that is required is that someone drop a small piece (or nidus) of ice into the water, and very quickly ice crystals will begin to form, and in a short time the liquid water will became solid ice.

On that "day of judgment" the prophetic movement may, like that small nidus of ice, function as a social "catalyst" in an unstable world, where perhaps even large numbers of God's true church, visible and invisible, reacting to and resisting the formation of Babylon, will "come out of her" to stand and be counted. We may well be utterly astonished by those we see coming out of the woodwork in that day. How many are out there who, like Nicodemus and Joseph of Arimathea, now seem apathetic, uncaring, and unresponsive to the prophetic message, but who are, in fact, waiting and growing? (It is very difficult to quantify the work of the Spirit.)

The point is that when the crucial time comes for releasing the winds of Revelation 7, God will need the right kind of people in the right places on earth to act as rallying foci for the gathering of the final remnant. When the "honest in heart" come out of Babylon and look around for the like-minded, they will need to know where to turn for identity, support, fellowship, and common struggle. Those who will fill that need will be those who are "sealed in their foreheads" — those who will understand and deliver an unmistakable picture of the truth about God and His way.

What God is waiting for during this time of holding back the winds, then, is for the right people to find their way to all the right places of earth. The establishment of that kind of presence is what constitutes the "finishing of the work." (By the way, if we feel free to identify the three angels of Revelation 14 as a human movement, we might well consider whether the four angels holding the winds [Rev. 7] may not also be so identified. Could Adventists have a four-angels' message as well as a three-angels' message to give to the world? Do we not have some responsibility for holding back the winds until the time?)

The "right place" includes the "tongues" of earth. "To every nation, kindred, tongue and people," and "tongues" could indicate more than traditional languages. Besides Tamil, Swahili, Tagalog, Spanish, and Russian, etc., the good news must become available to those who speak the languages of science, of art, of business, and of industry too. And "people" could mean the many "people groups" of the world, even if not necessarily every individual person in them.

The prophetic movement must be strengthened by as many faithful members as it can possibly win and become established as a presence in all these "right places" of the world. God alone will know when it is the right time to allow the storm to break, thrusting the two kingdoms into sharpest contrast before the universe. When this has taken place, the judgment will have been set, and soon it will all be over and our Lord will take His people home. When God has the right people in the right places, it will be the right time. And none of us can know the time before it is time. Could it be today or tomorrow? It is not for us to know.

Summary

How shall we now pull this all together? As we have noted, the Seventh-day Adventist movement, at least in the First World, may be facing its greatest crisis since the disappointment of 1844. There the question was one of *arrival*—of being born. Today's crisis is one of *survival* as a force in the world—of keeping alive. In a way it is a kind of midlife crisis—that time in life when individuals come to realize that their powers are waning; that they aren't really going anywhere; that their youthful dreams are never going to be realized; that others seem to be taking over, getting the promotions and choice assignments. And they take a look in the mirror. (It has frequently been noted that movements go through changes analogous to the life history of an individual person.)

What we face is a crisis of identity. We were once so sure of who we were and why we were here. We referred to ourselves in terms that seemed arrogant to others but expressed our own sense of God's special calling. This sense of specialness was the source of our considerable influence on the present world and filled us with hope for the future.

Some of what we thought about ourselves was unrealistic. And we matured. We came to realize that we couldn't do it all by ourselves, and that there were others besides ourselves who were special and felt special. And we may have lost something in that realization.

This book has been concerned about that loss and has suggested ways in which our special identity can be recaptured. We have proposed that what is necessary, first of all, is that we face up realistically to the logistics and other facts. One way to do this is to redefine ourselves. Rather than attempting to buttress our sagging sense of identity with illusions of an exclusive grasp of truth, as in "true church," we should be concentrating on mission. A people may be called prophetically—called to be God's mouthpiece and not His treasure. We are a prophetic movement and not God's "true church" in this sense. God's true church is bigger than anything humans beings can turn into an exclusive institution.

A prophetic movement derives its mission and reason for being from its message. To be true to God's call, then, this movement should be clear about what it has to say. This includes truths that we share with all Christians as Christians. But it especially concerns those truths that represent truth's progression at its growing edge. Such truth will continue to develop while it maintains continuity with its roots.

We have attempted to explore what God is doing in the world under the rubric of the three-angels' message of Revelation 14. This is the prophetic movement's message for our day. The three-angels' message represents a synthesis of ideas, tying together a call to worship the one God who, as Creator and Sustainer of all that is, imprints His own oneness on the whole. His sovereignty as our Creator is underscored by respect for His creation, for our own bodies, for the world around us, and for His Sabbath as a creation in time. It is also expressed in the way we go about our ordinary work.

The synthesis relates God's creative grace, His forgiveness, to the removal of guilt and to a renewal—a new creation—expressed as obedience and faith. This is a gospel for "every nation, tribe, language and people." It is primarily a message about God, about His kingdom locked in contest with the kingdom of Satan, a message in which the true nature of each is revealed for the universe to see. This conflict takes place in "time"—a time of judgment in which the final phase of that time is coincident with the birth of a prophetic movement.

It is also a message of assurance, assurance of the reality of forgiveness underscored by the acceptance of our alter ego, our heavenly High Priest before the "mercy seat" of Heaven. The revelation of the truth about God also allows the universe, including the redeemed, to "investigate" the moral validity of God's saving grace to its satisfaction.

What more can we say? All the above are couched in "ant language"—metaphor, symbols, figures of speech, analogies, parables—appropriate to the subject matter. Whenever God has communicated timeless truths, He has used such vehicles in order to allow for progression in understanding (our problem). This means that each generation can and must take a fresh look at the ways their fathers perceived and expressed things.

Above all, a prophetic movement must maintain an openness to new truth. It hasn't all been said yet. There needs to be a clear twenty-eighth doctrine added to the 27. It should read something like "This is as far as we have gone. There is more." It is in faithfulness to what we have received while we look for that "more" that this movement may keep alive and come victoriously through the crisis it now faces.

May God give it the wisdom to know how to do this, but even more the courage that the doing of it will surely require.

A final parable. (My former students will remember this.) There once were three peas who lived in pod. They looked at each other and at the walls of their pod and decided that the whole world was green. Summer slipped away, fall came, and the pod split wide open. To their dismay, the peas discovered that not only was the whole world not green, but that most of it was varying shades of brown. There were even some other shades of green. In panic, one pea took hold of the edges of the pod and tried to pull them back together again so that its world could be all green again. A second pea slipped out of the pod and became just as brown as it could as fast as it could so that no one would notice. The third pea looked at the walls of the pod and at the brown and green world outside and decided that its particular shade of green was precisely what the world out there needed.

And that's the way it is. God bless!

Bibliography

Introduction:

Hoffer, Eric. *The True Believer.* New York: Harper & Row, 1951.

Loma Linda University Church. *Dialogue,* October 1991, p. 3.

Seventh-day Adventists Answer Questions on Doctrine. Washington, D.C.: Review and Herald Pub. Assn., 1957.

Chapter 1:

Pegis, Anton C. *The Basic Writings of Saint Thomas Aquinas.* New York: Random House, 1944. Vol. I.

Chapter 2:

Buck, Pearl. *All Under Heaven.* New York: John Day, 1973.

Ehrlich, Paul. *The Population Bomb.* New York: Ballantine, 1968.

Robinson, D. E. *The Story of Our Health Message,* Nashville: Southern Pub. Assn., 1965.

Chapter 3:

Durant, Will. *The Story of Philosophy.* New York: Simon and Shuster, 1951.

Chapter 4:

Glasser, Arthur F. "A Friendly Outsider Looks at Seventh-day Adventists." *Ministry,* January 1989, p. 9.

Kübler-Ross, Elisabeth. "Death Does Not Exist." *The Journal of Holistic Health,* 1977, p. 9.

Chapter 5:

Otto, Rudolph. *The Idea of the Holy.* New York: Oxford Univ. Press, 1958.

Phillips, J. B. *Your God Is Too Small.* New York: Macmillan, 1954.

Snyder, Howard. *The Radical Wesley.;* Downers Grove, Ill.: Inter-Varsity Press, 1980.

Chapter 6:

Dawn, Marva. *Keeping the Sabbath Wholly.* Grand Rapids: Eerdmans, 1989.

Chapter 7:

Menninger, Karl. *Whatever Became of Sin?* New York: Hawthorn Books, Inc., 1973.

Thielemann, Bruce. *Christianity Today,* Oct. 7, 1991, p. 30.

Chapter 8:

Anselm of Canterbury. *Cur Deus Homo?* The Library of Christian Classics. Philadelphia: Westminster Press, 1956. Vol. X.

Harrington, Wilfred. *The Prodigal Father.* Wilmington, Del.: Michael Glazier, Inc., 1982.

Marshall, John C. "The Face of Justice." *Nature,* 337, No. 16 (February 1989): 607.

Time, Jan. 9, 1984, p. 28.

Chapter 9:

Richardson, Alan, ed. *A Theological Word Book of the Bible.* New York: Macmillan Co., 1950.

Chapter 10:

Chalmers, Thomas. In *Mead's Encyclopedia of Religious Quotations.* Old Tappen, N.J.: Fleming H. Revell Co.

Moody, Raymond A., Jr., *Life After Life.* Covington, Ga.: Mockingbird Books, 1976.

Tillich, Paul. "The Meaning of Health." *Perspectives in Biology and Medicine,* Autumn 1961.

Chapter 11:

Speiser, E. A., trans. *The Anchor Bible. Genesis.* Garden City, N.Y.: Doubleday & Co., 1964.

Chapter 12:

Dostoevsky, Fyodor. *The Brothers Karamazov.* Trans. Constance Garnett. New York: Random House.

Grier, Phillip T. "Something New Under the Tsars." *Science* 18 (August 1989): 769.

Heilbroner, Robert L. *An Inquiry Into the Human Prospect.* New York: W. W. Norton & Co., 1974.

Kass, Leon R. "What's Wrong With Babel?" *The American Scholar,* Winter 1989, pp. 41ff.

Kaufmann, Walter. *The Portable Nietzsche.* New York: Viking Press, 1954.

Sales, Stephen M., "Authoritarianism." *Psychology Today,* November 1972, p. 94.

Shirer, William L. *The Nightmare Years.* Boston: Bantam Books, 1985.

Stein, George J. "Biological Science and the Roots of Nazism." *American Scientist,* January-February 1988, pp. 50ff.

Thompson, William Irwin. In *Quest,* May/June, 1977, p. 92.

Time, July 3, 1989, p. 48.

Chapter 13:

Christianity Today, Aug. 29, 1975, p. 42.

One more thing about that ice analogy. David N. Spergel and Neil G. Turok tell us, "When water freezes suddenly, it does not form a perfect crystal; it is riddled with imperfections. These defects appear because as the water begins to freeze, tiny crystals of ice start growing throughout it. Each crystal assumes a random orientation as it forms. The crystals grow until they meet one another and fill all the available space. Defects in the crystal structure appear where regions of different orientations meet. The quicker the liquid cools, the more defects form, because the ice crystals have less time to grow before they encounter one another" ("Textures and Cosmic structure," *Scientific American,* March 1992, p. 55). Could it be that the rapidity of the final movements will result in relatively unimportant variations in culture, concepts, and lifestyle within the larger harmony of the "remnant" at the end?